The Norton Scores

NINTH EDITION | VOLUME 1

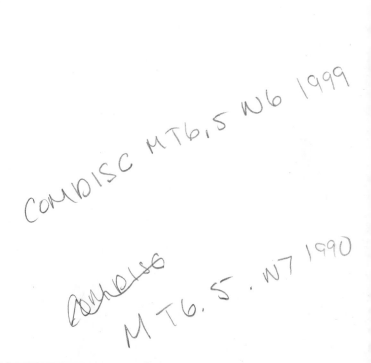

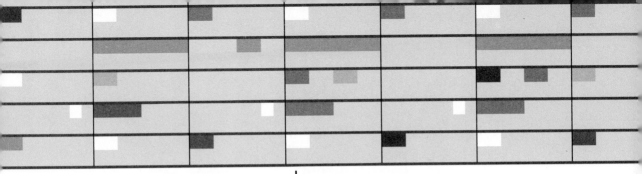

NINTH EDITION | IN TWO VOLUMES

The Norton Scores

A Study Anthology
Edited by Kristine Forney

Professor of Music
California State University, Long Beach

with textual notes
by Roger Hickman

Professor of Music
California State University, Long Beach

VOLUME 1: GREGORIAN CHANT
TO BEETHOVEN

W. W. NORTON & COMPANY
NEW YORK & LONDON

Composition by UG / GGS Information Services, Inc.
Manufacturing by Maple-Vail
Copy Editor: Jan Hoeper
Project Editor: Claire McCabe
Cover illustration: Helmut Preiss, *Jazz*, 1997.

ISBN 0-393-97945-8 (pbk.)

W. W. Norton & Company, Inc., 500 Fifth Avenue, New York, N.Y. 10110 www.wwnorton.com

W. W. Norton & Company Ltd., Castle House, 75/76 Wells Street, London W1T 3QT

1 2 3 4 5 6 7 8 9 0

Contents

Preface   ix

How to Follow the Highlighted Scores   xii

A Note on the Recordings   xiv

A Note on the Performance Practice of Early Music   xv

1. GREGORIAN CHANT, (10th century), Kyrie   1

2. HILDEGARD VON BINGEN (1098–1179), *Alleluia, O virga mediatrix (Alleluia, O mediating branch)*   3

3. NOTRE DAME SCHOOL (early-13th-century), Organum, *Gaude Maria virgo (Rejoice Mary, virgin)*, excerpt   8

4. ADAM DE LA HALLE (c. 1237–c. 1287), Motet, *Aucun se sont loé/ A Dieu/Super te (There are those who praise/To God/Above you)*   10

5. MONIOT D'ARRAS (fl. 1213–1239), *Ce fut en mai (It happened in May)*   14

6. GUILLAUME DE MACHAUT (c. 1300–1377), *Puis qu'en oubli (Since I am forgotten)*   18

7. ANONYMOUS (late 13th century), *Royal estampie* No. 4   20

8. GUILLAUME DU FAY (c. 1397–1474), *L'homme armé* Mass *(The Armed Man* Mass), Kyrie   22

9. JOSQUIN DES PREZ (c. 1450–1521), *Ave Maria . . . virgo serena (Hail Mary . . . gentle virgin)*   29

10. JOSQUIN, Chanson, *Mille regretz (A thousand regrets)*   38

11. TIELMAN SUSATO (c. 1515–c. 1571), Pavane *Mille regretz*   41

12. GIOVANNI PIERLUIGI DA PALESTRINA (c. 1525–1594), *Pope Marcellus* Mass, Gloria   43

Contents

13. GIOVANNI GABRIELI (c. 1557–1612), *O quam suavis* (*O how sweet*)   51

14. CLAUDIO MONTEVERDI (1567–1643), *A un giro sol*
(*At a single turning glance*)   61

15. MONTEVERDI, *L'incoronazione di Poppea (The Coronation of Poppea)*, Act III, Scene 7   67

16. JOHN FARMER (fl. 1591–1601), *Fair Phyllis*   77

17. BARBARA STROZZI (1619–after 1664), *Begli occhi* (*Beautiful Eyes*)   82

18. ARCANGELO CORELLI (1653–1713), Trio Sonata, Op. 3, No. 2
     Third movement   90
     Fourth movement   91

19. HENRY PURCELL (1659–1695), *Dido and Aeneas*, Act III, Dido's Lament   94

20. ANTONIO VIVALDI (1678–1741), *La primavera*, from *Le quattro stagioni* (*Spring*, from *The Four Seasons*)
     First movement   98
     Second movement   109
     Third movement   113

21. GEORGE FRIDERIC HANDEL (1685–1759), *Water Music*, Suite in D major
     Allegro   128
     Alla hornpipe   133

22. HANDEL, *Messiah*
     No. 1. Overture   140
     Nos. 14–16. Recitative, "There were shepherds abiding in the field"   146
     No. 17. Chorus, "Glory to God"   148
     No. 18. Aria, "Rejoice greatly"   153
     No. 44. Chorus, "Hallelujah"   159

23. JOHANN SEBASTIAN BACH (1685–1750), Chorale Prelude, *Ein feste Burg ist unser Gott* (*A Mighty Fortress Is Our God*)   170

24. BACH, *Brandenburg Concerto* No. 2 in F major
     First movement   175
     Second movement   195

25. BACH, Prelude and Fugue in C minor, from *The Well-Tempered Clavier*, Book I   199

26. BACH, Cantata No. 80, *Ein feste Burg ist unser Gott* (*A Mighty Fortress Is Our God*)
     No. 1. Choral fugue   204
     No. 2. Duet   231
     No. 5. Chorus   239
     No. 8. Chorale   257

27. JOHN GAY (1685–1732), *The Beggar's Opera*, end of Act II   260

28. FRANZ JOSEPH HAYDN (1732–1809), Symphony No. 94 in G major
    (Surprise), Second Movement   265

29. HAYDN, String Quartet, Op. 76, No. 2 *(Quinten)*,
    Fourth Movement   278

30. HAYDN, *Die Schöpfung (The Creation)*, Part I
    No. 12. Recitative, "Und Gott sprach, Es sei'n Lichter"   287
    No. 13. Recitative, "In vollem Glanze"   288
    No. 14. Chorus, "Die Himmel erzählen"   290

31. WOLFGANG AMADEUS MOZART (1756–1791), Piano Sonata in
    A major, K. 331, Third Movement   304

32. MOZART, Piano Concerto in G major, K. 453
    First movement   309
    Second movement   341
    Third movement   352

33. MOZART, *Le nozze di Figaro (The Marriage of Figaro)*
    Overture   378
    Act I, Scene 6: Aria, "Non so più"   400
    Act I, Scene 6: Recitative, "Ah, son perduto!"   407
    Act I, Scene 7: Terzetto, "Cosa sento!"   415

34. MOZART, *Eine kleine Nachtmusik (A Little Night Music)*, K. 525
    First movement   433
    Second movement   440
    Third movement   445
    Fourth movement   446

35. MOZART, Symphony No. 40 in G minor, K. 550, First Movement   456

36. LUDWIG VAN BEETHOVEN (1770–1827), Piano Sonata in C minor,
    Op. 13 *(Pathétique)*
    First movement   483
    Second movement   490
    Third movement   493

37. BEETHOVEN, Violin Concerto in D major, Op. 61, Third Movement   500

38. BEETHOVEN, Symphony No. 5 in C minor, Op. 67
    First movement   524
    Second movement   554
    Third movement   575
    Fourth movement   594

Appendix A. Reading a Musical Score   661

Appendix B. Instrumental Names and Abbreviations   663

Appendix C. Glossary of Musical Terms Used in the Scores   668

Appendix D. Concordance Table for Recordings and Listening Guides   676

Acknowledgments   679

Index of Forms and Genres   682

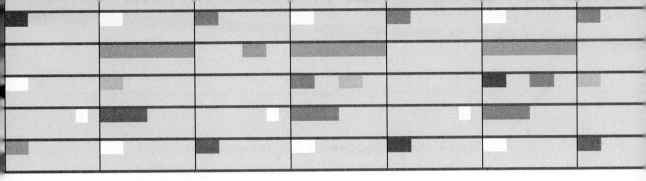

Preface

The Ninth Edition of *The Norton Scores* provides a comprehensive approach to the study of the masterworks of Western music literature, from the earliest times to the present. Presented in two volumes, the anthology meets a number of teaching and study needs in the field of music, including the following:

- as a core anthology, or an ancillary, for a masterworks-oriented music class, to aid in the development of listening and music-reading skills;
- as a study anthology for a music history class focused on major repertory, genres, or styles of Western music;
- as a core repertory for analysis classes, providing a wide variety of styles, forms, and genres;
- as a central text for a capstone course in musical styles focused on standard repertory, listening, or score study;
- as an ancillary to a beginning conducting course and a help in reading full orchestral scores;
- as an independent study resource for those wishing to expand their knowledge of repertory and styles;
- as a resource for music teachers in a wide array of courses.

The Norton Scores can be used independently, as described above, or in conjunction with an introductory music text. The repertory coordinates with *The Enjoyment of Music*, Ninth Edition, by Joseph Machlis and Kristine Forney. Recording packages are available for use with this edition: 8 CDs (in two volumes matching the contents and division of the score volumes) and 4 CDs (selected works).

The anthology presents many works in their entirety; others are represented by one or more movements or an excerpt. Most selections are reproduced in full scores; however, opera excerpts are given in piano/vocal scores. (In the case of some contemporary pieces, issues of copyright and practicality prevent the inclusion of a complete score.) Translations are provided for all foreign-texted vocal works, and each score is followed by an informative text that provides historical and stylistic information about the work.

The full scores in this anthology employ a unique system of highlighting that directs those who are just developing music-reading skills to preselected elements in the score, thus enhancing the music-listening experience. Students with good music-reading skills will, of course, perceive many additional details. Each system (or group of staves) is covered with a light gray screen, within which the most prominent musical lines are highlighted with white bands. Where two or more simultaneous musical lines are equally prominent, they are both highlighted. Multiple musical systems on a page are separated by a thin white band. For more information, see "How to Follow the Highlighted Scores" on p. xii. This highlighting system has been applied to most instrumental works in full scores; in vocal works, the text generally serves as a guide throughout the work.

The highlighting is not intended as an analysis of the melodic structure, contrapuntal texture, or any other musical aspect of the work. Since it emphasizes the most prominent line (or lines), however, it often represents the principal thematic material in a work. In some cases, the highlighting may shift mid-phrase to another instrument that becomes more audible.

Here are some considerations regarding the repertory included in this anthology:

- Music is divided into two volumes:
  - Volume I: Gregorian Chant to Beethoven
  - Volume II: Schubert to the Present
  - 8-CD set matches this division
- All major Classical genres are represented:
  - New genres in this edition include Baroque trio sonata, Italian cantata, nocturne, Mexican art music, prepared piano, spiritual minimalism
  - Complete multi-movement works for study (Baroque concerto, Classical symphony, concerto, chamber music, sonata)
- Seven works by women composers:
  - Middle Ages to contemporary (Hildegard von Bingen, Barbara Strozzi, Clara Schumann, Fanny Mendelssohn Hensel, Amy Cheney Beach, Billie Holiday, Joan Tower)
  - Wide-ranging genres (chant, Italian cantata, piano music, song, chamber music, jazz, orchestral music, among others)

- Numerous works influenced by traditional and world musics:
    - Traditional music of the Americas (Ives song, Copland ballet, Revueltas symphonic work, Bernstein musical theater work, Cajun dance tune)
    - European traditional music (Haydn quartet, Gay ballad opera, Bizet opera, Ravel orchestral work)
    - Eastern influence (Mozart sonata, Puccini opera, Mahler song cycle, Cage prepared piano work)
    - African influence (Ligeti piano etude, jazz selections)

The appendices to *The Norton Scores* provide some useful pedagogical resources for students and faculty. These include the following:

- table of clefs and instrument transpositions;
- table of instrument names and abbreviations in four languages (English, Italian, German, and French);
- table of voice designations in English, Italian, and Latin;
- table of scale degree names (in four languages);
- glossary of all musical terms in the scores;
- table of concordances between scores, recordings, and listening guides in *The Enjoyment of Music;*
- index by genre and form of all selections in the anthology.

Volume I also has a helpful explanation of some performance practice issues in early music, and, where needed, editor's notes explain particular markings in a score that might not be widely understood.

There are many people to be thanked for help in the preparation of this Ninth Edition of *The Norton Scores*: my California State University, Long Beach colleagues Roger Hickman, for his informative texts on each musical selection, and Gregory Maldonado, for his expert work on the highlighting of new scores; research assistants Carla Reisch, Denise Odello, Patricia Dobiesz, and Jeanne Scheppach, for their invaluable help on this project; John Muller of The Juilliard School of Music, for his assistance in the coordination of the scores with the recordings; Claire McCabe and Allison Benter, both of W. W. Norton, who ably collected the scores and handled the permissions; Jan Hoeper, for her capable copyediting of the scores and texts; Kathy Talalay of W. W. Norton, for her skillful and painstaking work on the entire *Enjoyment of Music* package; and Maribeth Payne, music editor at W. W. Norton, for her support and guidance of this new edition. I am deeply indebted to them all.

How to Follow the Highlighted Scores

By following the highlighted bands throughout a work, the listener will be able to read the score and recognize the most important or most audible musical lines. The following principles are illustrated on the facing page in an excerpt from Beethoven's Symphony No. 5 in C minor (first movement).

1. The musical line that is most prominent at any time is highlighted by a white band shown against light gray screening.
2. When a highlighted line continues from one system (group of staves) or page to the next, the white band ends with an arrow head (>) that indicates the continuation of the highlighted line, which begins on the next system with an indented arrow shape.
3. Multiple systems (more than one on a page) are separated by narrow white bands across the full width of the page. Watch carefully for these bands so that you do not overlook a portion of the score.
4. At times, two musical lines are highlighted simultaneously, indicating that they are equally audible. On first listening, it may be best to follow only one of these.
5. When more than one instrument plays the same musical line, in unison or octaves (called doubling), the instrument whose line is most audible is highlighted.
6. CD track numbers are given throughout the scores at the beginning of each movement and at important structural points within movements. They appear in a ☐ for the 8-CD set and in a ◇ for the 4-CD set, where appropriate.

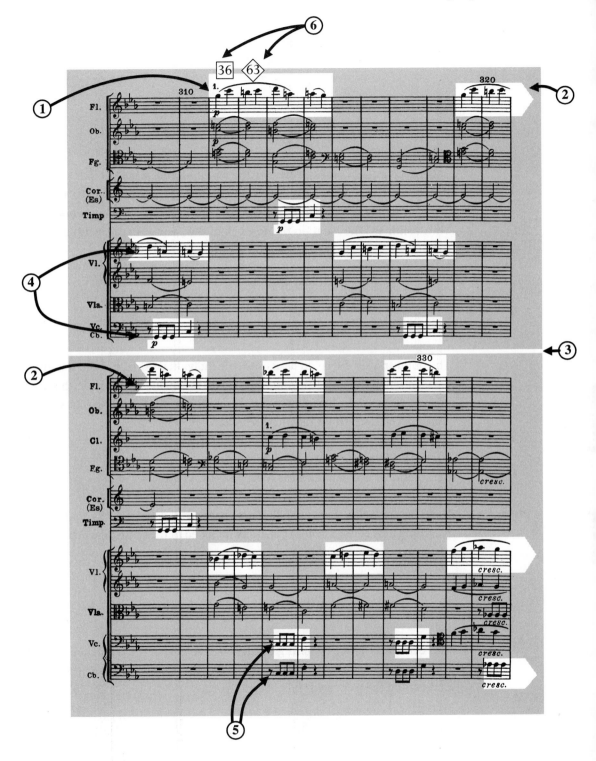

A Note on the Recordings

Sets of recordings of the works in *The Norton Scores* are available from the publisher. There is an 8-CD set that includes all the works in the two volumes of the anthology and a 4-CD set that includes selected works from both volumes. The location of the work in the recording sets is noted at the top of each score, to the right of the title.

Example (for Schubert's *Erlkonig*)
8CD:5/ 1 – 8
4CD:1/ 80 – 87

The number after the colon designates the individual CD within the set; the boxed numbers after the diagonal slash gives the inclusive tracks on that CD. For an overview of which works appear on the various recording sets, see Appendix D *Concordance Table for Recordings*.

For the 8-CD set, the first set accompanies *The Norton Scores*, Volume I, and the second set accompanies *The Norton Scores*, Volume II.

Note: Occasionally, there are differences between the notated scores and the recordings; an editor's note is generally included in the score to explain these performance choices.

Electronic Listening Guides

There are interactive Listening Guides available from the publisher for each work on the 8-CD and 4-CD sets. These provide study tools to help students understand the form and style of each work.

A Note on the Performance Practice of Early Music

In recordings of early music, you may observe that performances vary somewhat from the printed score. These variants reflect changing interpretations of the performance practices of the era. Also, because early notation was not as precise as that of modern times, certain decisions are left to the performer. Thus, there is no one "correct" way to perform a work.

1. Before around 1600, the decision to use voices or instruments and the choice of specific instruments were largely up to the performers. Thus, a vocal line may be played rather than sung, may alternate between voices and instruments, or may be sung with instruments doubling the part. In instrumental music, modern performances may vary widely in the choice of instruments used.

2. In some of the earliest pieces, precise rhythmic interpretation is open to question. Bar lines, which were not used in early notation, have been added to most modern scores to facilitate metric interpretation.

3. In early notated music, the placement of words in relation to notes was rarely precise, leaving the text underlay to the performers. A modern edition presents one possible solution to the alignment of the words to the music, while a recording may present another possibility. Since languages were not standardized in early times, modern editions often maintain the text spellings of the original source, and performers sometimes follow historical rules of pronunciation.

4. Accidentals were added to medieval and Renaissance music by performers, according to certain rules. In modern scores, these accidentals (called *musica ficta*) are either shown above the notes or on the staff in small type, as performance suggestions. Other editorial additions to scores are generally printed in italics (such as tempo markings and dynamics) or placed between square brackets.

5. In Baroque music, figured bass (consisting of a bass line and numbers indicating the harmonies to be played on a chordal instrument) was employed as a kind of shorthand from which musicians improvised, or "realized," the accompaniment at sight. In some modern scores, a

suggested realization is provided by the editor, although performers may choose to play their own version of the accompaniment.

6. It was standard practice in music from the medieval to Classical periods to improvise accompaniments and to add embellishments to melodic lines, especially in repetitions of musical material. Today's performers often attempt to recreate the sound of this spontaneous style.

7. In earlier times, pitch varied according to the performance situation and the geographic locale. Modern replicas of historical instruments often sound at a lower pitch than today's standard (A = 440), and musicians occasionally choose to transpose music to a higher or lower key to facilitate performance.

1. Gregorian Chant

Kyrie (10th Century)

KYrie * e- lé- i-son. *iij.* Chrí- ste e-

lé- i-son. *iij.* Ký- ri- e e- lé- i-son. *ij.* Ký-ri- e *

e- lé- i-son.

Editor's note: In this example from the *Liber usualis,* the number above the first initial indicates the chant is in mode 8, or hypomixolydian; the *iij* in the text is a repeat *(iterum)* sign, signifying that the text is sung three times; and the asterisk (*) signals a choral response.

1. Gregorian Chant, Kyrie

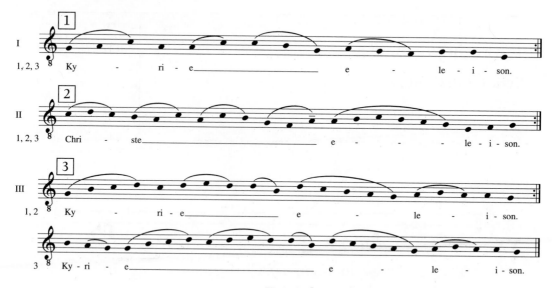

Text and Translation

Kyrie eleison.	Lord, have mercy upon us.
Kyrie eleison.	Lord, have mercy upon us.
Kyrie eleison.	Lord, have mercy upon us.
Christe eleison.	Christ, have mercy upon us.
Christe eleison.	Christ, have mercy upon us.
Christe eleison.	Christ, have mercy upon us.
Kyrie eleison.	Lord, have mercy upon us.
Kyrie eleison.	Lord, have mercy upon us.
Kyrie eleison.	Lord, have mercy upon us.

The Kyrie is the first portion of the Mass service after the opening processional (Introit). The text consists of a threefold repetition of three acclamations: "Kyrie eleison"(Lord, have mercy upon us), "Christe eleison"(Christ, have mercy upon us), and "Kyrie eleison" (Lord, have mercy upon us). These words are sung in every Mass service; the Kyrie, then, is the first section of the Mass Ordinary.

The musical setting maintains the tripartite division of the text: **A-A-A B-B-B C-C-C'**. Moving primarily with conjunct motion (stepwise), the entire melody lies within the range of an octave. Typical of tenth-century Kyries, each successive section increases in range, and the Christe and second Kyrie are both extended by melismas (singing of many notes to a single syllable). In keeping with standard performance practices, the chant is sung monophonically without a strict metric pulse. The alternation between a soloist and a choir, as heard in the recording, is called responsorial singing.

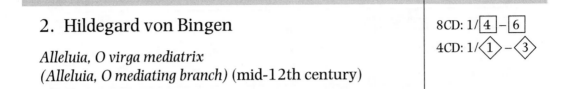

2. Hildegard von Bingen

Alleluia, O virga mediatrix
(Alleluia, O mediating branch) (mid-12th century)

2. Hildegard von Bingen, *Alleluia, O virga mediatrix*

Editor's note: In this transcription, slurs show compound neumes (or signs denoting multiple notes); small notes show a particular kind of single neume (diamond-shaped in the original notation), and slashed eighth notes show a passing note that should be only half-vocalized, or sung lightly. Because there are differing manuscript sources for this chant, the recording varies slightly from the original notation shown here and the transcription.

2. Hildegard von Bingen, *Alleluia, O virga mediatrix*

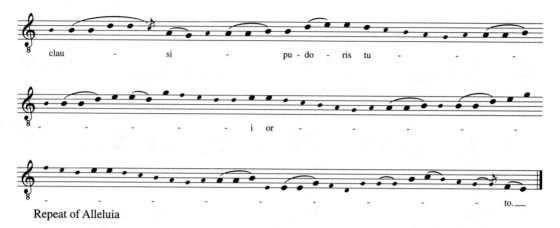

clau - si - pu - do - ris tu - - -

- - - - i or - - - -

- - - - - - - - to.___

Repeat of Alleluia

Text and Translation

Alleluia
O virga mediatrix
sancta viscera tua mortem superaverunt,
et venter tuus omnes creaturas illuminavit

in pulchro flore de suavissima integritate

clausi pudoris tui orto.
Alleluia.

Alleluia.
O mediating branch
Your holy flesh has overcome death,
And your womb has illuminated all
      creatures
Through the beautiful flower of your tender
      purity
That sprang from your chastity.
Alleluia.

Hildegard von Bingen (1098–1179) is one of the most fascinating figures of the Middle Ages. A visionary, composer, and writer of science, philosophy, poetry, and drama, she founded her own convent in Rupertsberg, Germany, and served as abbess there. Her twelfth-century Alleluia provides a beautiful example of the late medieval style and of Hildegard's remarkable talents as a poet and composer.

The Alleluia follows the Gradual in the Mass service and is part of the musical response to the Scripture lessons. The text can be seen in an **A-B-A** pattern; the **A** portions contain the single word "Alleluia," and the **B** presents a Verse that is appropriate to the particular feast day. Since this text changes for every service, the chant is part of the Mass Proper.

Musical settings of Alleluias generally retain the **A-B-A** structure of the text and follow a traditional pattern of responsorial singing (alternating soloist and choir). The Alleluia begins with an intonation by a soloist. The chorus then repeats the opening phrase and continues with a lengthy melisma on the last syllable (*-ia*), called a *jubilus*. The Verse is sung either by a soloist with a brief choral response or by the soloist without a response, as in this example. At the return of the Alleluia, the chorus repeats the opening phrase and the *jubilus*.

Hildegard's Verse, which reflects the late medieval fascination with the Virgin Mary, pays homage and joyful reverence to Christ's Mother. The initial section is primarily set in a neumatic manner and does not venture far from the *finalis* (final tone). But with the references to "holy womb," "flower," and "chasity," Hildegard supports these images with extended melismas, an expanded range, and her signature leaps of a fifth. The melody dramatically climaxes on a G, which is heard twice at the parallel melismas for "tui" and "orto." Hildegard gives the entire work a sense of unity by making several melodic references to the Alleluia, most notably at the beginning and end of the Verse. Since Hildegard's chants were likely sung at her convent, performances by women were considered acceptable in her day, as they are today.

3. Notre Dame School (early-13th century)

Organum, *Gaude Maria virgo (Rejoice Mary, virgin)*, excerpt

* Norton recording fades out here.

Text and Translation

Gaude Maria	Rejoice Mary,
virgo cunctas hereses sola	O virgin, you alone have
interemisti.	destroyed all heresies.

❦

The earliest examples of polyphony, called *organum*, appear in the Gradual and Alleluia from the Mass and the Responsory from the Offices. All three chants are responsorial, both in their function as a musical response to Scripture readings and in their performance practice of alternating solo and choral sections (the choir literally responds to a soloist). Polyphony appears only during the solo passages of these chants.

A significant repertory of such works was created at the Notre Dame Cathedral in Paris during the twelfth and thirteenth centuries. Distinctive of Notre Dame polyphony is the addition of between one and three quickly moving melodic lines over the long, sustained notes of the original chant. The Responsory *Gaude Maria virgo (Rejoice Mary, virgin)* is sung at Vespers and Matins for the Purification of the Virgin (February 2) and at Matins for the Feast of Circumcision (January 1). In this excerpt, the opening solo intonation is set in polyphony, while the chorus portion, beginning with the word "virgo," is sung in monophonic chant. In the solo section, the original chant is in the bottom voice (Tenor), and the newly composed upper voices (Duplum and Triplum) sing an extended melisma with a strong rhythmic pulse. This three-part polyphonic texture is typical of the thirteenth-century style of Pérotin. Based on the repetitive pattern of a rhythmic mode, the upper voices primarily alternate between long and short notes. The Duplum and the Triplum have similar ranges and frequently interchange material.

4. Adam de la Halle

Motet, *Aucun se sont loé/ A Dieu/ Super te (There are those who praise/ To God/ Above You)* (13th Century)

4. Adam de la Halle, *Aucun se sont loé/ A Dieu/ Super te*

Text and Translation

Triplum

Aucun se sont loé d'amours,
Mais je m'en doi plus que nus blasmer,
C'onques a nul jour
N'i poi loiauté trouver.
Je cuidai au premiers
Avoir amie par loiaument
Ouvrer,
Mais g'i peüsse longuement
Baer,
Car quant je miex amai,
Plus me convient maus endurer,
N'onques chele que j'amoie,
Ne me vaut maustrer
Sanlant ou je me deüsse conforter
Ne merchi esperer,
Tout adès metoit paine a moi eskiever;
Trop m'i donna a penser
Ains que je le peüsse ouvlier.
Or voi je bien sans douter
Que loiaus hom est perdus qui veut amer,
Ne nus, che m'est vis, ne s'en doit mesler
Fors cil qui bée a servir de guiller.

There are those who praise love
but I must curse it more than anyone,
for not even for one day
have I found loyalty.
I thought at first
that, through loyalty, I would
win love,
but I would have had to wait
forever,
for the more faithful I was
the more pain I had to endure.
For she whom I loved
never granted me
a comforting glance
nor gave me any hope,
she took great pains to avoid me;
she gave me much trouble
by the time I could forget her.
Now I see perfectly
that a faithful man is lost if he wants love,
no one, in my opinion, should get involved
unless he too is served by deceit.

Duplum

A Dieu commant amouretes
Car je m'en vois
Doulans pour les douchetes,
Fors dou douc païs d'Artois,
Qui est si mus et destrois
Pour che que li bourgois
Ont esté si fourmené
Qu'il n'i queurt drois ne lois,

To God I commend my loves
for I must go away
lamenting the sweet things,
far away from the land of Artois,
which is so silent and anguished
because its people
have been so afflicted
that they no longer have courts, nor rights,
nor laws.

Gros tournois
Ont anulés
Contes et rois,
Justiches et prelas, tant de fois
Que mainte bele compaigne,
Dont Arras mehaingne,
Laissent amis et maisons et harnois,
Et fuient, cha deus, che trois,
Souspirant en terre estrange.

The grand tournaments
have been canceled
by counts and kings,
judges and prelates, so often
that many of the fine people,
those whom Arras scorns,
have left their friends, homes, and belongings,
and flee, in twos and threes,
sighing, for a foreign land.

Tenor

Super te

Above you

Aucun se sont loé/A Dieu/Super te (There are those who praise/ To God/ Above you) is one of five motets ascribed to Adam de la Halle (c. 1237–c. 1287). Like the other four, this polytextual motet is set with two melodic lines over a Gregorian chant Tenor. The Tenor, performed by a bowed string instrument on the recording, maintains a consistent pulse, with alternating long and short notes. The rhythm consists of small repeating units that can be described as a rhythmic ostinato.

The upper voices share the same general range and move in quicker rhythmic values. Each of the upper two voices is a setting of a French poem. *Aucun se sont loé* is a lover's lament. The poet has been faithful and patient, but this has only brought on pain and suffering. In light of the Duplum text, this complaint takes on a subtle political meaning.

A Dieu commant amouretes borrows its opening and closing lines (shown in italics in the score) from the refrains of a secular rondeau composed by Adam de la Halle bearing the same title. The standard rondeau images of love give way to an expression of sorrow over the political situation in the region of Artois (in Northern France near the English Channel) and the treatment of its people by those from Arras, the principal city in this region. A score of the earlier rondeau can be seen in *The New Grove Dictionary of Music and Musicians* (Nigel Wilkens, "Rondeau (i)").

5. Moniot d'Arras

Ce fut en mai (It happened in May)
(mid-13th century)

Nonmeasured Transcription

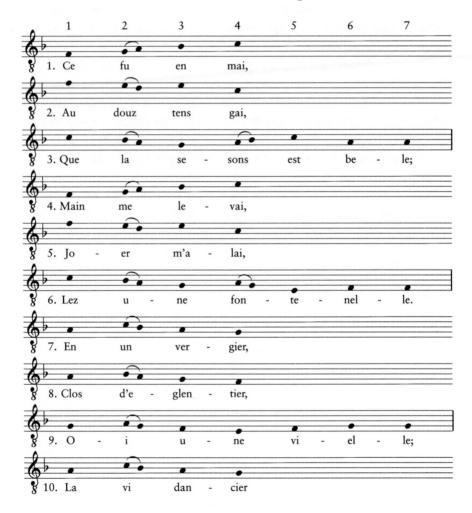

Editor's note: Text and spellings in these transcriptions reflect variants in the original sources. In the Norton recording, the measured transcription is sung, with improvised instrumental accompaniment.

11. Un che - va - lier

12. Et u - ne da - moi - se - le.

Measured Transcription

A
Ce fut en mai Au douz tens gai Que la sai-sons est be - le;
Main me le-vai Jo - er m'a-lai Lez

u - ne fon - te - ne - le.

B
En un ver- ger Clos d'es-glen-tier O - i u-ne vi - e - le;
La vi dan-cer Un che - va-lier Et

u - ne de - moi - se - le.

Text and Translation

11	I.	Ce fut en mai

I. Ce fut en mai It happened in May
Au douz tens gai When skies are gray
Que la saisons est bele, And green the plains and mountains,
Main me levai, At break of day
Joer m'alai I rose to play
Lez une fontenele. Beside a little fountain.
En un vergier In garden close
Clos d'aiglentier Where shone the rose
Oi une viele; I heard a fiddle played, then
La vi dancier A handsome knight
Un chevalier That charmed my sight
Et une damoisele. Was dancing with a maiden.

5. Moniot d'Arras, *Ce fut en mai*

12   II.   Cors orent gent   Both fair of face,

Cors orent gent	Both fair of face,
Et avenant,	They turned with grace
Et molt très bien dançoient;	To tread their Maytime measure;
En acolant	The flowering place,
Et en baisant	Their close embrace,
Molt biau se deduisoient.	Their kisses, brought them pleasure.
Au chief du tor,	Yet shortly they
En un destor,	Had slipped away
Doi et doi s'en aloient;	And strolled among the bowers;
Le jeu d'amor	To ease their heart
Desus la flor	Each played the part
A lor plaisir faisoient.	In love's games on the flowers.

13   III.

J'alai avant,	I crept ahead
Molt redoutant	All chill with dread
Que nus d'aus ne me voie,	Lest someone there should see me,
Maz et pensant	Bemused and sad
Et desirrant	Because I had
D'avoir ausi grant joie.	No joy like theirs to please me.
Lors vi lever	Then one of those
Un de lor per	I'd seen there, rose
De si loing com j'estoie	And from afar off speaking
Por apeler	He questioned me
Et demander	Who I might be
Qui sui ni que queroie.	And what I came there seeking.

14   IV.

J'alai vers aus,	I stepped their way
Dis lor mes maus,	To sadly say
Que une dame amoie,	How long I'd loved a lady
A cui loiaus	Whom all my days
Sans estre faus	My heart obeys
Tot mon vivant seroie,	Full faithfully and steady,
Por cui plus trai	Though still I bore
Peine et esmai	A grief so sore
Que dire ne porroie.	In losing one so lovely.
Et bien le sai,	That surely I
Que je morrai,	Would come to die
S'ele ne mi ravoie.	Unless she deigned to love me.

15   V.

Tot belement	With wisdom rare,
Et doucement	With tactful air,
Chascuns d'aus me ravoie.	They counseled and relieved me.
Et dient tant	They said their prayer
Que Dieus briement	That God might spare
M'envoit de celi joie	Some joy in love that grieved me
Por qui je sent	Where all my gain

Paine et torment:	Was loss and pain,
Et je lor en rendoie	So I, in turn, extended
Merci molt grant	My thanks sincere
Et en plorant	With many a tear
A Dé les comandoie.	And them to God commended.

Moniot d'Arras (fl. 1213–39) was a monk associated with the abbey of St. Vaast in Arras in Northern France. Although he composed some sacred works, he is best known as a poet and composer of secular chansons in the trouvère tradition. Dating from the early-to-mid-thirteenth century, *Ce fut en mai (It happend in May)* is a monophonic song set in strophic form. The folklike melody contains two pairs of phrases, creating an **A-A-B-B** pattern. Exhibiting characteristics of the *pastourelle,* the poem deals with images of nature and the poet's observations on the love between a knight and a young woman. The quasi-religious ending may be due to the composer's position as a monk. Paul Hindemith quotes this melody in his ballet *Nobilissima visione.* In this recording, an accompaniment to the melody is improvised by three string instruments: a psaltery, which is plucked; a dulcimer, which uses hammers; and a bowed vielle. Between the verses, the vielle inserts a fragment of the principal melody.

6. Guillaume de Machaut

Puis qu'en oubli (Since I am forgotten)
(mid-14th century)

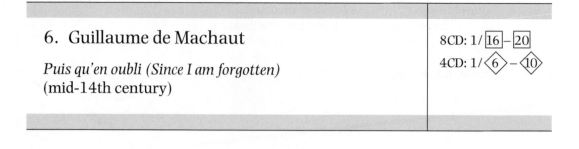

Editor's note: The numbers next to the text signal the order in which to perform the two sections of the rondeau. The bracketed notes were originally written as ligatures—notational devices that combined two or more notes into a single symbol.

Text and Translation

16	6	Refrain	Puis qu'en oubli sui de vous, dous amis, Vie amoureuse et joie a Dieu commant.	Since I am forgotten by you, sweet friend, I bid farewell to a life of love and joy.
17	7	Verse	Mar vi le jour que m'amour en vous mis;	Unlucky was the day I placed my love in you;
18	8	Partial refrain	Puis qu'en oubli sui de vous, dous amis.	Since I am forgotten by you, sweet friend.
19	9	Verse	Mais ce tenray que je vous ay promis: C'est que jamais n'aray nul autre amant.	But what was promised you I will sustain: That I shall never have any other love.
20	10	Refrain	Puis qu'en oubli sui de vous, dous amis, Vie amoureuse et joie a Dieu commant.	Since I am forgotten by you, sweet friend, I bid farewell to a life of love and joy.

Guillaume de Machaut (c. 1300–1377), who achieved greatness in both poetry and music, can be seen as a late-medieval counterpart to the troubadours and trouvères. At the same time, his polyphonic secular music looks forward to the chanson of the early Renaissance. Machaut was a key figure in establishing the fixed poetic forms that would dominate secular music for over a century. The rondeau *Puis qu'en oubli (Since I am forgotten)* exhibits the standard **A-B-a-A-a-b-A-B** structure associated with the poetic genre. The subject is a traditional theme of courtly love—unrequited and unhappy love. But Machaut's reiterated refrains of "Since I am forgotten by you, sweet friend" and "I bid farewell to a life of love and joy" create an added poignancy and sense of pain.

Also indicative of future developments is the three-part texture. The setting with the principal melody in the top line accompanied by two lower lines will remain in vogue in secular music until the time of Josquin. The low range of the principal melodic line suggests a performance either by three men or by a solo male voice with instrumental accompaniment. The angular melodies and the prominent double-leading-tone cadence at the end of the **B** section are distinctive of the fourteenth century.

Royal estampie No. 4

Editor's note: Ornamentation and parallel harmony heard on the Norton recording are improvised by the performers.

The *Royal estampie* No. 4 has a simple structure that facilitates improvisation. The work is divided into seven sections, each of which contains a brief melodic idea that is repeated with alternating cadences. The two cadential phrases begin with the same four measures, but they differ in length and final pitch. The phrase leading to an open cadence on A has seven measures, while the answering phrase ending in a closed cadence (on the home pitch F) has eight. Since the pair of cadential phrases is the same for each section, the overall form can be diagrammed: 1x1y 2x2y 3x3y 4x4y 5x5y 6x6y 7x7y.

The melody has a limited range and could be performed by any number of melodic instruments. In the recording, the cadential phrases are consistently performed by shawms and percussion. The other solo instruments include a three-holed pipe, a rebec, and vielles. While the performance retains the basic monophonic texture of the original dance tune, variety is provided by the addition of ornamentation, drones, and parallel melodic movement.

8. Guillaume Du Fay

L'homme armé Mass *(The Armed Man* Mass*)*,
Kyrie (1460s)

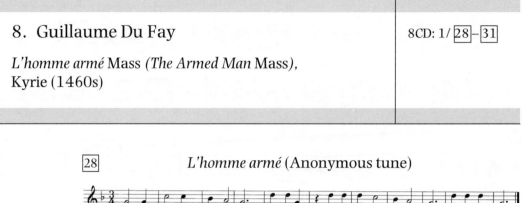

28   *L'homme armé* (Anonymous tune)

Text and Translation

L'homme, l'homme, l'homme armé,	The armed man,
L'homme armé doibt on doubter.	The armed man is to be feared.
On a fait partout crier	The cry has been raised all around,
Que chascun se viengue armer	that everyone should arm himself
D'un haubregon de fer.	with an iron hauberk [coat of mail].
L'homme, l'homme, l'homme armé	The armed man,
L'homme, armé doibt on doubter.	The armed man is to be feared.

Kyrie

8. Guillaume Du Fay, *L'homme armé* Mass: Kyrie

Text and Translation

Kyrie I

Kyrie, eleison.	Lord, have mercy upon us.
Kyrie, eleison.	Lord, have mercy upon us.
Kyrie, eleison.	Lord, have mercy upon us.

Christe

Christe, eleison.	Christ, have mercy upon us.
Christe, eleison.	Christ, have mercy upon us.
Christe, eleison.	Christ, have mercy upon us.

Kyrie II

Kyrie, eleison.	Lord, have mercy upon us.
Kyrie, eleison.	Lord, have mercy upon us.
Kyrie, eleison.	Lord, have mercy upon us.

In the early Renaissance, composers began setting the five principal sections of the Mass Ordinary as a cycle, unified by a common melody called a *cantus firmus* (literally "fixed melody") in the Tenor of each section. Du Fay (c. 1397–1474) is one of the first composers to use the secular tune *L'homme armé* (*The Armed Man*) as a cantus firmus for a cyclic Mass. The tune, set with long rhythmic values, appears in the Tenor line throughout the Mass and provides a structural framework for each movement. In the Kyrie, the tune's tripartite form **(A-B-A)** coincides with the three sections of the Kyrie, with slight modifications. In each of the three sections, the entrance of the Tenor is delayed, creating a reduced voicing that expands with the entrance of the cantus firmus. The duetting nature of the upper voices, which is most prominent at the opening of the Christe, is primarily set in nonimitative counterpoint.

Other early Renaissance features can be observed. The *a cappella* setting for four voices, the triadic passing harmonies, and the emphasis on counterpoint (primarily nonimitative) reflect the new style of the fifteenth century. Ties to the medieval past can be seen in the perfect harmonies at major cadences, the similarity of the four vocal ranges (all sung by men), and the melodic dominance of the upper voices.

9. Josquin des Prez

Ave Maria . . . virgo serena (Hail Mary . . . gentle virgin) (1480s?)

9. Josquin des Prez, *Ave Maria . . . virgo serena*

Text and Translation

Ave Maria, gratia plena,	Hail Mary, full of grace,
Dominus tecum, virgo serena.	The Lord is with you, gentle Virgin.
Ave cujus conceptio	Hail, whose conception,
Solemni plena gaudio	Full of solemn joy,
Caelestia, terrestria,	Fills the heaven, the earth,
Nova replet laetitia.	With new rejoicing.
Ave cujus nativitas	Hail, whose birth
Nostra fuit solemnitas,	Was our festival,
Ut lucifer lux oriens,	As our luminous rising light
Verum solem praeveniens.	Coming before the true sun.
Ave pia humilitas,	Hail, pious humility,
Sine viro fecunditas,	Fertility without a man,
Cujus annuntiatio,	Whose annunciation
Nostra fuit salvatio.	Was our salvation.
Ave vera virginitas,	Hail, true virginity,
Immaculata castitas,	unspotted chastity,
Cujus purificatio	Whose purification
Nostra fuit purgatio.	Was our cleansing.
Ave praeclara omnibus	Hail, famous with all
Angelicis virtutibus,	Angelic virtues,
Cujus fuit assumptio	Whose assumption was
Nostra glorificatio.	Our glorification.
O Mater Dei,	O Mother of God,
Memento mei.	Remember me.
Amen.	Amen.

The Renaissance motet, unlike its medieval counterpart, is a setting of a single text on a sacred subject in Latin. In its broadest definition, the term can be applied to any polyphonic composition based on a Catholic Latin text other than the Ordinary of the Mass. The text of the motet *Ave Maria . . . virgo serena* (*Hail Mary . . . gentle virgin*) by Josquin des Prez (c. 1450–1521) is a Latin poem praising the Virgin Mary. Consisting of an opening couplet, five quatrains, and a closing couplet, the poem contains a simple rhyme scheme. The acclamation "Ave" is the initial word for the opening couplet and for all five quatrains.

The repetitive structure of the poem is reflected in the music, but Josquin's mastery of Renaissance style creates a continuous, nearly seamless flow. Although this motet is intended for male voices (ideally *a cappella*), the vocal ranges are more distinct than those in Du Fay's Mass. The bass voice has been extended lower, and the top voice would have been sung by boy sopranos. Josquin creates variety by alternating chordal and imitative textures and by continuously changing the number and combination of voices. The texture is frequently divided between the two upper voices and the two lower voices, and these pairs alternate in imitative fashion. Also striking is the fourth quatrain (beginning in m. 47), which is set in a chordal texture, yet contains a canon separated by one beat between the soprano and tenor. Indicative of the early date for this work (probably from the 1480s), the major cadences still close with open-fifth harmonies.

10. Josquin des Prez

Chanson, *Mille regretz (A thousand regrets)* (1520)

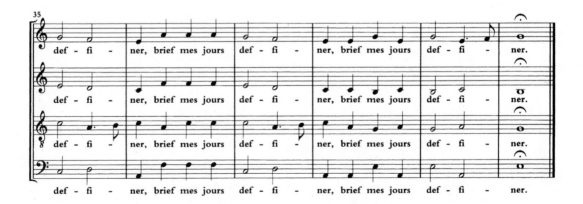

10. Josquin des Prez, *Mille regretz*

Text and Translation

Mille regretz de vous habandonner	A thousand regrets for deserting you
Et d'eslonger vostre fache amoureuse,	And leaving behind your loving face,
Jay si grand dueil et paine douloureuse,	I have such great sorrow and grievous pain,
Qu'on me verra brief mes jours definer.	That one can see that my dayswill not be long.

Mille regretz (*A thousand regrets*), which may have been written for Charles V in 1520, exemplifies the Renaissance conception of the secular song. Abandoning the fixed poetic forms of the late Middle Ages, Josquin sets a simple four-line love poem. The treble-dominated three-part texture characteristic of earlier secular songs gives way to an expressive four-part setting. Since the work is secular, performances could have involved female singers and instrumentalists. In this recording, the *a cappella* ideal is retained.

Although much of *Mille regretz* displays a homorhythmic texture, each voice plays an independent role in the work as a whole. The chanson presents several points of imitation, either involving all four voices (mm. 24–27) or pairs of voices (mm. 19–24). The use of overlapping cadences allows the music to flow without breaks until the closing section (m. 34), which echoes the final phrase of the poem three times. Josquin creates a pervading sense of sadness in this work through the continuously descending melodic phrases and the choice of Phrygian mode.

11. Tielman Susato

Pavane *Mille regretz* (published 1551)

This arrangement of Josquin's chanson appears in a collection of dances published by Tielman Susato (c. 1515–c. 1571) in Antwerp in 1551. Taking the form of a pavane, one of the most popular dance types of the sixteenth century, the work exhibits the characteristic moderate tempo, duple meter, and sectional structure associated with the dance. The arranger has skillfully molded the seamless flow of the original chanson into a three-part structure, each with a repeated eight-measure phrase.

The Pavane *Mille regretz (A thousand regrets)*, like the original chanson, is set for four parts. At times, such as at the beginning, the lower lines are similar to the corresponding lines of the original. But for the most part, the lower lines are relegated to harmonic support. No instruments are specified in the published dance, and the limited ranges (generally within an octave) allow for a variety of instrumental combinations. In this recording, violas da gamba and a lute play the first statement of each section, and an organ and recorders join on the repeat. A tabor (drum) provides a rhythmic accompaniment.

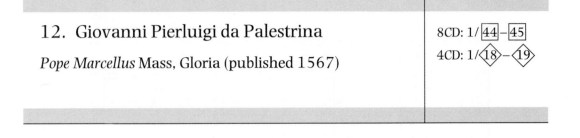

12. Giovanni Pierluigi da Palestrina

Pope Marcellus Mass, Gloria (published 1567)

8CD: 1/ 44 – 45

4CD: 1/ 18 – 19

Text and Translation

Gloria in excelsis Deo	Glory be to God on high,
et in terra pax hominibus	and on earth peace to men
bonae voluntatis.	of good will.
Laudamus te,	We praise Thee.
Benedicimus te.	We bless Thee.
Adoramus te.	We adore Thee
Glorificamus te.	We glorify Thee.
Gratias agimus tibi propter	We give Thee thanks for
magnam gloriam tuam.	Thy great glory.
Domine Deus, Rex caelestis,	Lord God, heavenly King,
Deus Pater omnipotens.	God the Father Almighty.
Domine Fili	O Lord, the only-begotten Son,
unigenite, Jesu Christe.	Jesus Christ.
Domine Deus, Agnus Dei,	Lord God, Lamb of God,

Filius Patris.	Son of the Father.
Qui tollis	Thou that takest away
peccata mundi,	the sins of the world,
miserere nobis.	Have mercy on us.
Qui tollis peccata mundi,	Thou that takest away the sins
suscipe deprecationem nostram.	Of the world, receive our prayer.
Qui sedes ad dexteram Patris,	Thou that sittest at the right hand
miserere nobis.	of the father, have mercy on us.
Quoniam tu solus sanctus.	For thou alone art holy.
Tu solus Dominus.	Thou only art the Lord.
Tu solus Altissimus.	Thou alone art most high.
Jesu Christe, cum Sancto Spiritu	Jesus Christ, along with the Holy Spirit
in gloria Dei Patris.	in the glory of God the Father.
Amen.	Amen.

Giovanni Pierluigi da Palestrina (c. 1525–1594), a composer of over one hundred Masses, can be seen as the foremost musical representative of the Counter-Reformation movement in Rome. Responding to the challenge of the Reformation, the Council of Trent suggested reforms for the Catholic Church, even focusing its attention on music. In particular, concerns were expressed about words being obscured by careless pronunciation and complicated counterpoint. According to a popular anecdote, the Council considered completely banning polyphony from services, but was convinced by the beauty and clarity of Palestrina's *Pope Marcellus* Mass (1567) to refrain from such action.

While the validity of the story is questionable, the resulting reputation has made this Mass one of the most celebrated sacred works of the era. The declamation of the text in the Gloria, primarily set in a six-part homophonic texture, certainly adheres to the guidelines of the Council. Variety is created through changes in register and in the number of voices singing at any given moment. The final "Amen" section contains the only suggestion of the pervasive imitative style that characterizes late Renaissance sacred music.

13. Giovanni Gabrieli

O quam suavis (O how sweet) (published 1615)

60
- tens i - na - nes, i - na - nes, i - na - nes,
di - mit - tens i - na - nes, i- na - nes,
- tens, di - mit - tens i - na - nes, i - na - nes,
- tens, di - mit - tens i - na - nes, i - na - nes,
- tens, di - mit - tens i - na - nes, i - na - nes, di- mit - -
- tens, di - mit - tens i - na - nes, i - na - nes, di-mit - -
- tens, di-mit-tens i - na - nes, i - na - nes, di- mit - -
- tens, di - mit - tens i - na - nes, i - na - nes, di-mit - -
di- mit - - tens i- na - nes, di - mit - -
di- mit . - - tens i - na - nes, di-mit - -
di-mit - - tens i - na - nes, di-mit - -
di - mit - - tens i - na - nes, di-mit - -
- tens i - na - nes, di - mit - - tens
- tens i - na - nes, di - mit - - tens
- tens, di -mit - - tens i - na - nes, di-mit - - tens
- tens, di-mit - - tens i - na - nes, di-mit - - tens

13. Gabrieli, *O quam suavis*

O quam suavis est, Domine, spiritus tuus;
qui, ut dulcedinem tuam
in filios demonstrares,
pane suavissimo de caelo praestito,
esurientes reples bonis,
fastidiosos divites dimittens inanes.

O how sweet, Lord, is your spirit,
who demonstrates your sweetness
to your sons
by providing the sweetest bread from heaven;
you fill the hungry with good things,
and send the rich and scornful away empty.

The transition from the Renaissance to the Baroque can most dramatically be seen in the polychoral motets of Giovanni Gabrieli (c. 1557–1612). While retaining some ties to the Renaissance style, Gabrieli moves away from the *a cappella* sound and pervasive imitation of the previous generation and exploits the potency of a newer, more homorhythmic musical style. *O quam suavis* (*O how sweet*), a setting of a text from the Vespers service for the Feast of Corpus Christe, was published posthumously in Gabrieli's second book of *Sacrae Symphoniae* (*Sacred Symphonies,* 1615). Reflecting the polychoral tradition associated with the St. Mark's Cathedral in Venice, the motet is divided into two choirs. Both contain four voices; the first choir is set for cantus (highest part), alto, tenor, and bass, and the second is set for a lower ensemble of alto, two tenors, and a bass. In keeping with appropriate performance practices, the recorded performance uses boy sopranos and sackbuts (similar to the modern trombones), which double a number of the lower vocal lines.

The change in musical conception can be seen in the more declamatory melodic style that sometimes creates a sense of dialogue between the two choirs. At times, the quick melodic turns and dotted rhythms suggest an instrumental, rather than vocal, conception. The strong emotional quality created by these brief motives, the antiphonal singing of the two choirs, and the chromatic harmonies point to the emerging Baroque style. Also indicative of the newer style are the mixture of voices and instruments and the presence of an organ basso continuo.

14. Claudio Monteverdi

A un giro sol (At a single turning glance)
(published 1603)

Text and Translation

A un giro sol de' bell' occhi lucenti,	At a single turning glance from those bright eyes
Ride l'aria d'intorno	the breeze laughs all about,
E'l mar s'acqueta e i venti	the sea becomes calm, then the wind dies away
E si fa il ciel d'un altro lume adorno;	and the sky becomes more radiant.
Sol io le luci ho lagrimose e meste.	I alone am sad and weeping.
Certo quando nasceste,	Doubtless on the day you were born,
Cosí crudel e ria,	so cruel and wicked,
Nacque la morte mia.	My death was also born.

Claudio Monteverdi's five-voice *A un giro sol* (*At a single turning glance*), published in his *Fourth Book of Madrigals* (1603), reflects a number of characteristics of the Renaissance madrigal. The variety of images provided by Giovanni Guarini's poem, which include joy, calm, radiance, and despair, are vividly reflected by Monteverdi (1567–1643) through word painting. In keeping with the Renaissance style, the upper four voices are essentially equal and often engage in imitative counterpoint.

A number of newer stylistic features are also evident in this work. The lively settings of the images of a turning glance, the laughing breeze, and the wind were inspired by the new virtuosic vocal style of the professional women singers from Ferrara, known as the Concerto delle donne. The bass line generally supports these melodic flights with a clear harmonic underpinning that is reinforced by an added *basso seguente* line. Also indicative of future developments is the recitative-like repetition of words on a single pitch following measure 43.

15. Claudio Monteverdi

L'incoronazione di Poppea (The Coronation of Poppea),
Act III, Scene 7 (1642)

Editor's note: In the Norton recording, the consuls and tribunes are sung as solos.
Throughout the score, footnotes refer to two manuscript sources, one in Naples (N),
and the other in Venice (V).

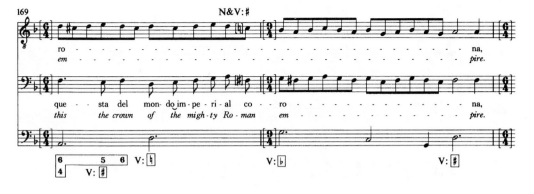

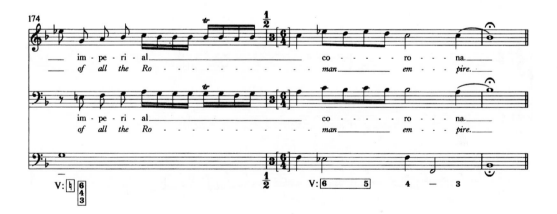

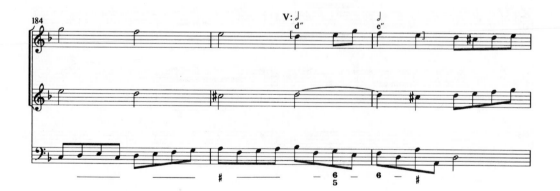

Editor's note: Norton recording omits the Ritornello (measures 339–343), but adds an instrumental introduction based on the ground-bass figure. The role of Nero, originally a castrato, is sung on the Norton recording by a mezzo-soprano.

Composed in the year prior to the composer's death, Monteverdi's *The Coronation of Poppea* (1642) stands as a masterpiece of early Baroque opera. The original final scene has been lost, and the version that comes down to us today is the product of revisions made by younger contemporaries. The libretto created by Giovanni Busenello deals with a historical episode in the unsavory life of the Roman emperor Nero. Seduced by the beauty and charms of the courtesan Poppea, Nero divorces his wife (and has her executed) in order to remarry. His principal adviser, the philosopher Seneca, is also condemned to death for his opposition to Nero's decision. The final coronation scene for Poppea may seem like the triumph of evil over good, but Monteverdi's audience would likely have known that Poppea was killed within three years, reportedly kicked to death in a fit of anger by Nero.

The coronation scene comprises two principal vocal sections. The first, an elaborate duet in which the consuls pay tribute to the new queen, contains both a recitative and an aria-like passage in triple meter. The elaborate cadential motion includes an example of *stile concitato* (agitated style), in which a single pitch is reiterated with rapid sixteenth notes. The second section, the final duet of the lovers Nero and Poppea, is an **A-B-B-A** pattern, a precursor to the da capo form **(A-B-A)** that will characterize Italian opera well into the eighteenth century. The **A** section features a four-note descending ground bass. In the recording, the basso continuo includes at various times a harpsichord, lute, and organ. Period instruments can also be heard in the three-part sinfonia that separates the two duets.

16. John Farmer

Fair Phyllis (published 1599)

8CD: 1/56

4CD: 1/20

Following the appearance of *Musica Transalpina* in 1588, madrigals became all the rage in England. The English madrigal differs from its Italian model in its generally lighter tone. Despite the presence of great English poets at the time, including Shakespeare, the choice of poetry does not match the high quality often found in Italian settings. Moreover, the texture tends to be more melodically oriented, with the principal musical interest lying in the top voice.

Fair Phyllis appears in John Farmer's only publication of four-part madrigals (1599). Following the tradition of the lighter madrigal style established by Thomas Morley, Farmer sets this idyllic poetic vision with contrasting homorhythmic and polyphonic sections. He creates a playful mood through word painting and subtle metric shifts, such as the delightful triple meter at the end. In the tradition of the Italian madrigal, the final line of text is repeated, which Farmer (fl. 1591–1601) uses to underscore the humor of his amorous word painting.

17. Barbara Strozzi

Begli occhi (Beautiful Eyes) (published 1654)

me- - no. Ahi, ahi ch'io vi ___ mo- ro, ahi

me- - no. ___ Ahi, ahi ch'io vi ___ mo- ro

ch'io vi ___ mo- ro, vi ___ mo- ro in ___ se- no,

in se- - no, vi ___ mo- ro, Ahi,

Ahi ch'io vi mo- ro ___ in se- no.

ahi ch'io vi mo- ro ___ in se- no. ___

Pen- sa- te che ___ fa- reb- bo- no,

Pen- sa- te che fa- reb- bo- no, Pen- sa- te che fa-

Pen- sa- te che fa- reb- bo- no Gli _____ stra- li si pun-

-reb- bo- no Gli _____ stra- li si pun- gen- ti,

-gen- ti, si pun- gen- ti, si pun- gen- ti e mor- ta-

si pun- gen- ti, si pun- gen- ti, si pun- gen- ti e mor- ta- li; __

-li; Lan- gue l'a- ni- ma,

_ Lan- gue l'a- ni- ma, lan- gue

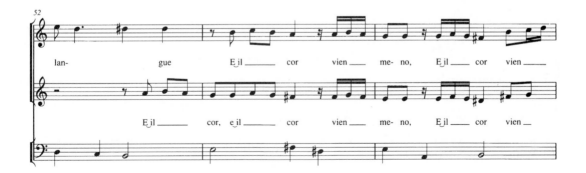

lan- gue E il ___ cor vien ___ me- no, E il ___ cor vien ___

E il ___ cor, e il ___ cor vien ___ me- no, E il ___ cor vien ___

Text and Translation

Mi ferite oh begli occhi	You wound me, oh beautiful eyes
Pensate che farebbono quei baci	Imagine what these kisses could do
Si cocenti e mardaci.	So burning and biting.
Langue l'anima e il cor vien meno	My soul languishes and my heart faints:
Ahi ch'io vi moro in seno!	Oh that I die there in my breast!
Pensate che farebbono gli strali;	Imagine what arrows could do;
Si pungente e mortali.	So sharp and deadly.
Langue l'anima e il cor vien meno	My soul languishes and my heart faints:
Ahi ch'io vi moro in seno!	Oh that I die there in my breast!
Ma forse non morrò senza vendetta;	But perhaps I will not die without revenge;
Ch'al fin chi morte da, la morte aspetta!	For he who deals death, awaits it in the end!

One of the musical innovations of the early Baroque period was a new vocal style called *monody*. Inspired by descriptions of Greek music, monody features an expressive solo melody with simple chordal accompaniment. Two distinct melodic styles can be observed in the monodies of the early seventeenth century: a freer, more expressive style similar to recitative and a more tuneful aria style. Both can be found in dramatic works (operas), sacred music, and in extended secular songs, which became known as *cantatas*. The accompaniment for monodies, played by a melodic bass instrument and an instrument capable of improvising chords from a figured bass line, is called the *basso continuo*. In the recording, the basso continuo is played by a cello and a harpsichord.

Begli occhi (*Beautiful Eyes*) by Barbara Strozzi (1619–1677), is a secular cantata published in 1654 for two high solo voices and basso continuo, a common texture in the Baroque era. Typical of the time, the cantata contains both recitative and aria styles. Three aria-like passages in triple meter can be heard: the two settings of the lines beginning with the word "pensate" (imagine) and the final duplet (m. 66). The other melodic material, set with a freer rhythmic pulse, tends to be more chromatic and dissonant. Particularly striking is the word painting for "Langue l'anima" ("my soul languishes"), which involves chromaticism and half-step movement. The end of the cantata presents a virtuosic display in the upper voices, as the poem closes with a delightful example of word painting (a lengthy melisma on "aspetta," suggesting the long wait for death) and visions of eternal retribution.

18. Arcangelo Corelli

Trio Sonata, Op. 3, No. 2 (published 1689)

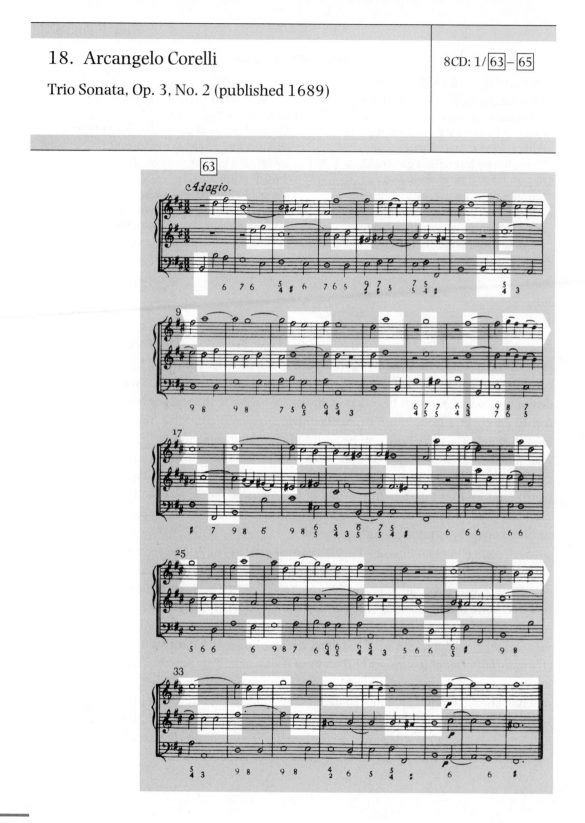

The trio sonata was one of the most common instrumental genres of the Baroque era. Primarily performed with two violins and a basso continuo (a cello with either a harpsichord or organ), these sonatas are set either as a series of dance movements (*sonata da camera*) or in a four-movement pattern of slow-fast-slow-fast (*sonata da chiesa*). Arcangelo Corelli (1653–1713), with four publications of twelve trio sonatas in each, can be seen as the foremost composer of the genre.

These two movements from his Op. 3, No. 2, are the second half of a *sonata da chiesa* structure. The Adagio exhibits the tempo and rhythmic gestures of a sarabande dance, but the form is continuous. While the upper voices alternate passages in imitation, parallel thirds, and chains of suspensions, the bass line primarily serves a harmonic function. The final cadence, offset with a hemiola, closes on the dominant of B minor and is never resolved, as the Allegro begins in D major.

The Allegro also suggests a dance rhythm—the gigue—and it is set in the standard binary form of the Baroque dance. A three-part fugal texture involving an active bass line can be heard throughout the movement. The second half begins with an inverted statement of the principal subject. The period instruments heard in the recording clearly delineate each line and create a warm, homogenous sound.

19. Henry Purcell

Dido and Aeneas, Act III, Dido's Lament
(1689)

8 CD: 1/ 66 – 68
4CD: 1/ 21 – 23

Dido and Aeneas, by Henry Purcell (1659–1695), is based on an episode in Virgil's *Aeneid,* in which the Trojan prince Aeneas pauses for a brief stay in Carthage, while on his journey to become the founder of Rome. He falls in love with the widowed Carthaginian queen Dido, but abandons her to fulfill his destiny. With his departure, Dido sings a final lament and dies in a burning funeral pyre. Since *Dido and Aeneas* was written for a performance at a boarding school for young women in 1689, the final "Remember me" would have been a clear moralizing message to the students.

After a brief recitative sung by Dido to her faithful serving maid Belinda, the aria begins with a chromatically descending ostinato theme in the bass. During the aria, the ground bass theme is heard eight times. The subtle overlapping of the phrases for the voice with the repetitions of the bass theme establishes a strong sense of continuity and creates numerous harmonic clashes that underscore Dido's pain. At the end of the aria, the orchestra repeats the theme twice more, with the addition of imitative chromatic descents in the upper strings.

20. Antonio Vivaldi

La primavera, from *Le quattro stagioni*
(*Spring*, from *The Four Seasons*)
(published 1725)

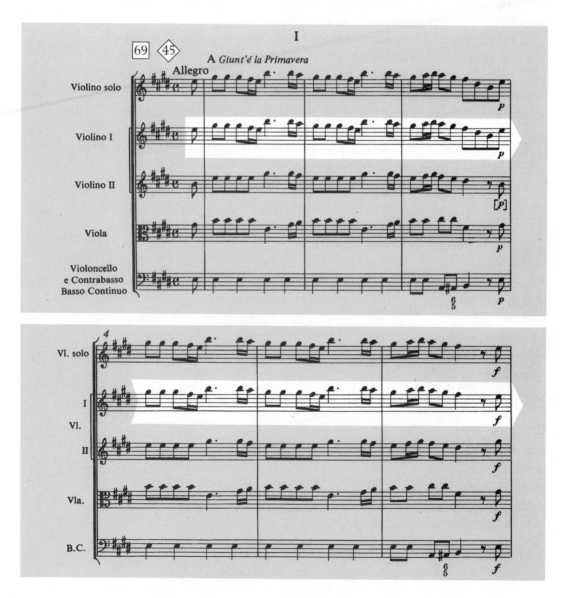

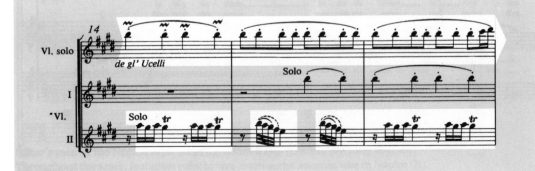

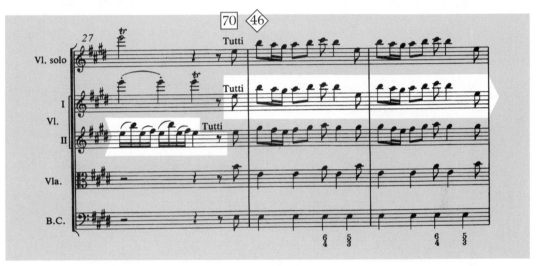

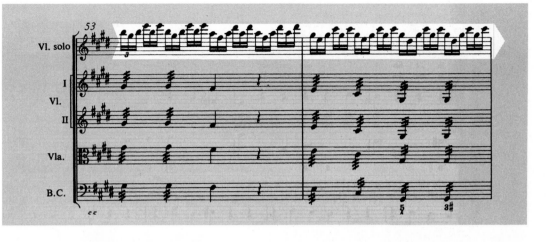

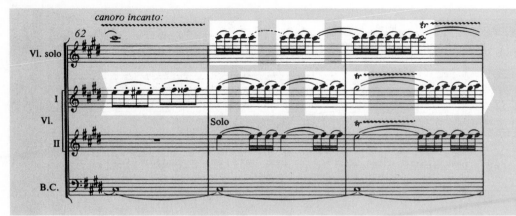

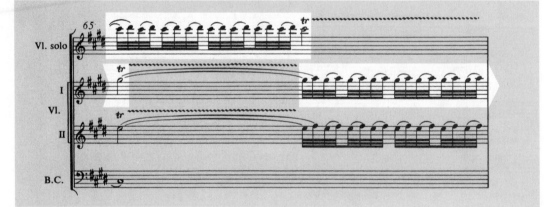

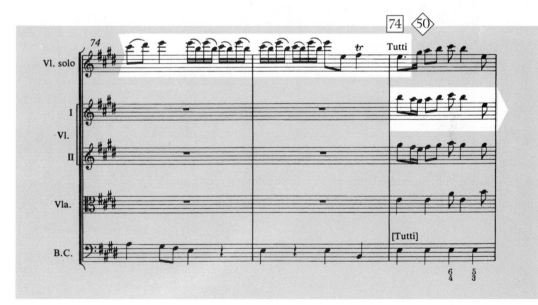

II

Editor's note: The continuation of the dotted pattern in measure 1 in Violin 1 and 2 is implied (usually marked *simile*). The viola instructions translate: "this should always be played very loud and strongly accented."

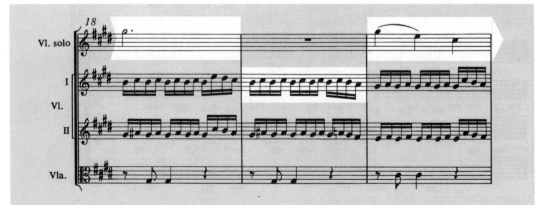

III

DANZA PASTORALE

Di pastoral Zampogna al Suon festante Danzan Ninfe e Pastor nel tetto amato

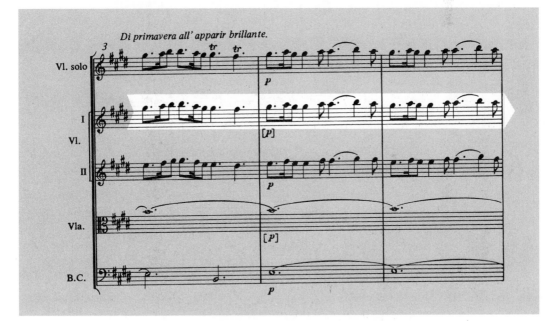

Di primavera all' apparir brillante.

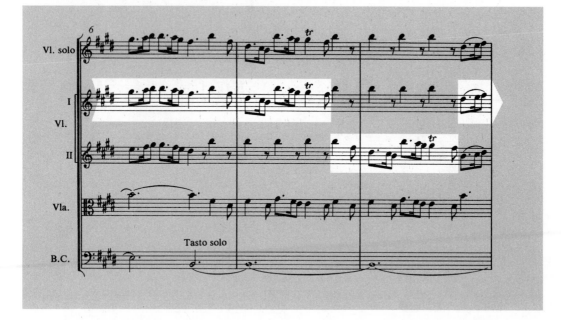

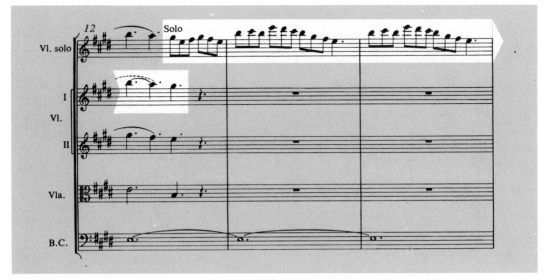

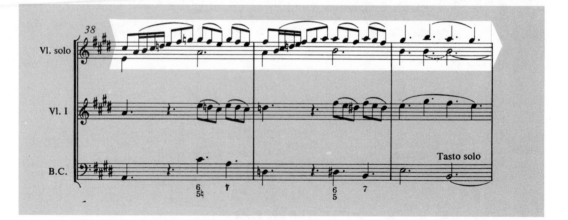

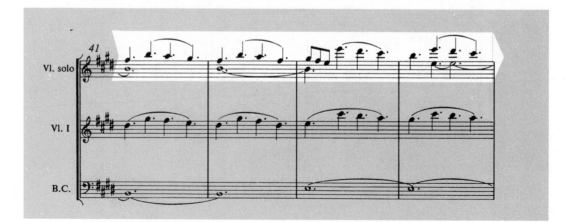

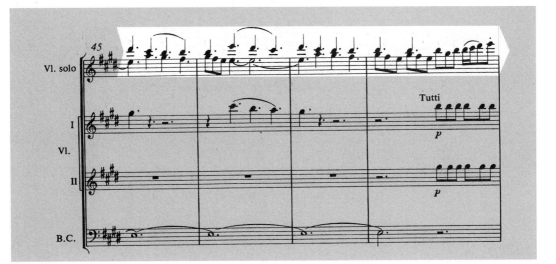

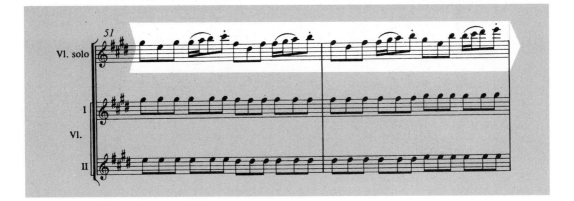

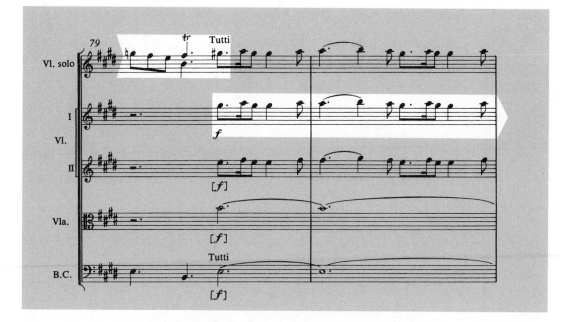

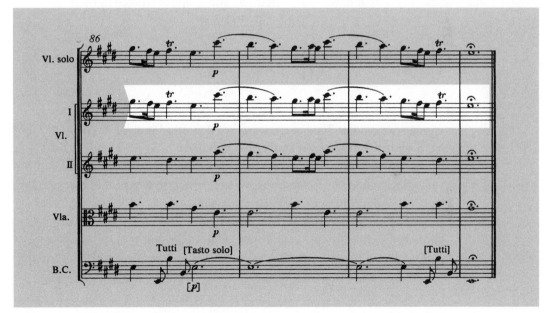

Text and Translation

I. Allegro

Giunt' è la Primavera e festosetti
la salutan gl'augei con lieto canto,
e i fonti allo spirar de'zeffiretti
con dolce mormorio scorrono intanto.

Joyful spring has arrived,
the birds greet it with their cheerful song,
and the brooks in the gentle breezes
flow with a sweet murmur.

Vengon' coprendo l'aer di nero amanto,
e lampi, e tuoni ad annuntiarla eletti.
Indi tacendo questi, gl'augeleti;
tornan' di nuovo allor canoro incanto:

The sky is covered with a black mantle,
and thunder and lightning announce a storm.
When they fall silent, the birds
take up again their melodious song.

II. Largo

E quindi sul fiorito ameno prato,
Al caro mormorio di fronde e piante,
Dorme'l caprar col fido can'a lato.

And in the pleasant, flowery meadow,
to the gentle murmur of bushes and trees,
the goatherd sleeps, with his faithful dog at
his side.

III. Allegro (*Rustic Dance*)

Di pastoral zampogna al suon festante
danzan ninfe e pastor nel tetto amato

To the festive sounds of a rustic bagpipe
nymphs and shepherd dance in their
favorite spot

di primavera all'apparir brillante.

when spring appears in its brilliance.

Le quattro stagioni (The Four Seasons) of Antonio Vivaldi (1678–1741) are his most celebrated violin concertos. Published in 1725 as Op. 8, Nos. 1–4, these programmatic concertos depict scenes in each of the seasons of the year. Interpolated onto the score of each concerto is a sonnet (presumably by Vivaldi) describing the particular season.

In *La primavera (Spring)*, the poem avoids any sense of narrative and is limited to general visions of spring. These pictorial images are presented within the framework of the solo violin concerto as established by Vivaldi. In addition to the three-movement format, the outer allegro movements retain ritornello structures. In the first movement, the orchestral ritornello statements are separated by episodes (often featuring a virtuoso solo violin part) that depict the sounds of birds, a murmuring brook, a storm, and birds again. The slow movement features a cantabile solo violin melody, which is performed with improvised embellishments in the recording. The warmth of tone created by the gut strings and Baroque bow enhances the tranquil mood. The orchestral accompaniment, which omits the lower strings and harpsichord continuo, is characterized by a repetitive dotted rhythm in the violins and a two-note figure in the violas that represents a barking dog *(il cane che grida)*. The dancelike ritornello theme of the third movement is set over a bagpipe-like drone in the lower strings. The orchestra ritornello and the solo sections, revealing a variety of solo/orchestra relationships, sustain the general image of joyful dancing. The period instruments heard in the recording create a clearly articulated sound that is particularly effective in passages with rapid notes, such as in the depiction of lightning and the subsequent flight of birds.

21. George Frideric Handel
Water Music, Suite in D major,
Allegro and Alla hornpipe (1717)

Allegro

Editor's note: In the Norton recording, timpani have been added. In the Baroque era,
the timpani functioned as the bass of the trumpet family.

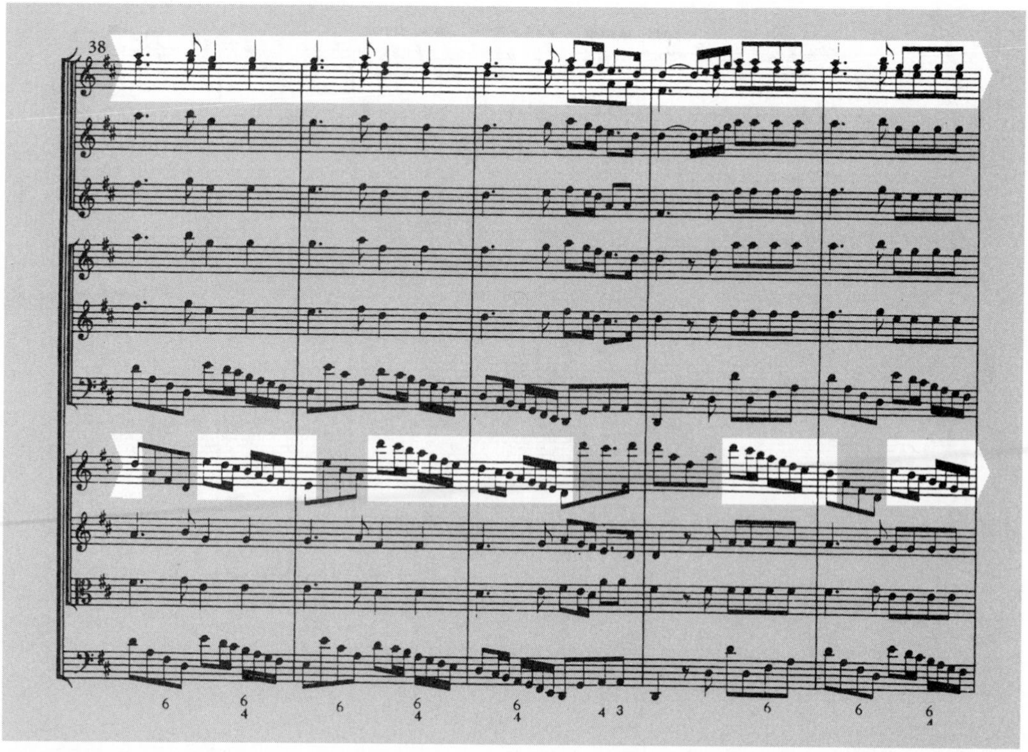
38
6 6/4 6 6/4 6/4 4 3 6 6 6/4

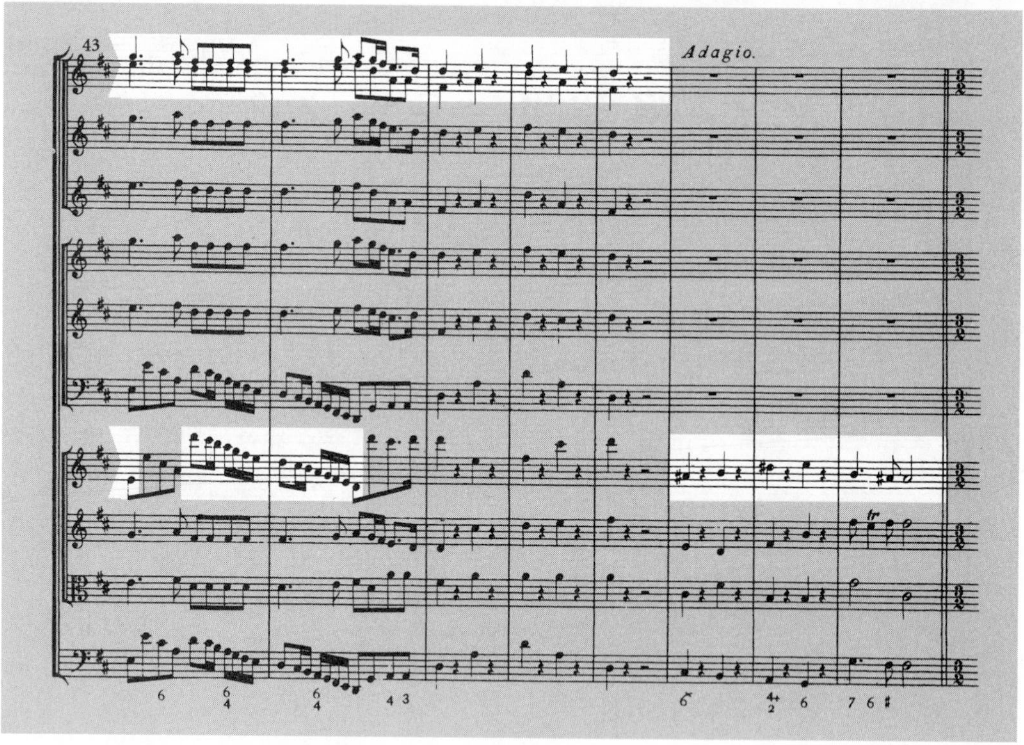
43
Adagio.
6 6/4 6/4 4 3 6 4+/2 6 7 6 ♯

Alla hornpipe

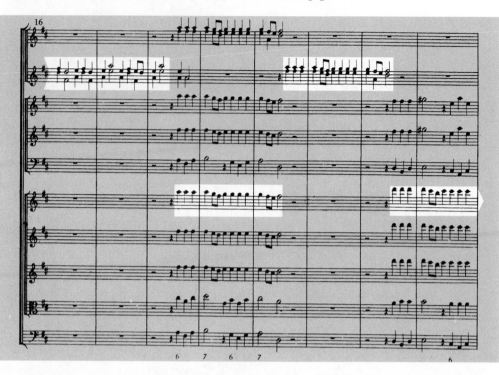

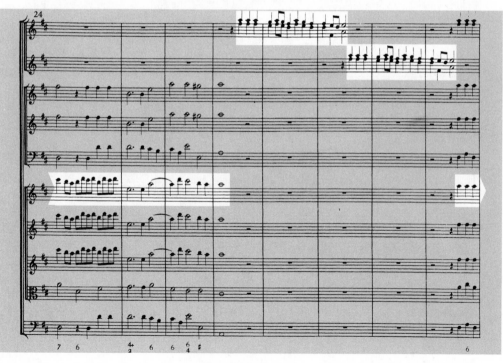

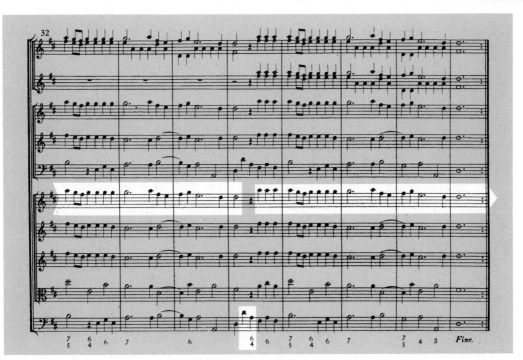

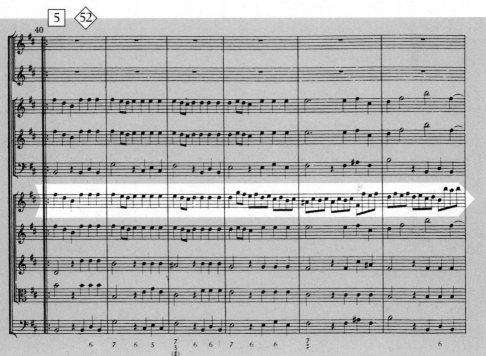

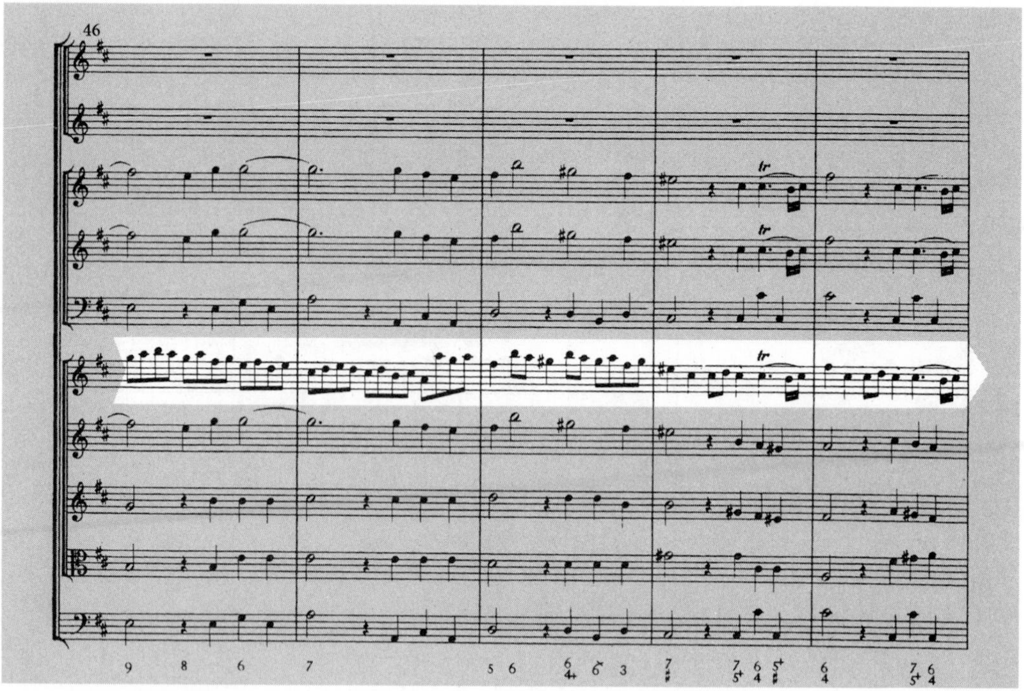
46

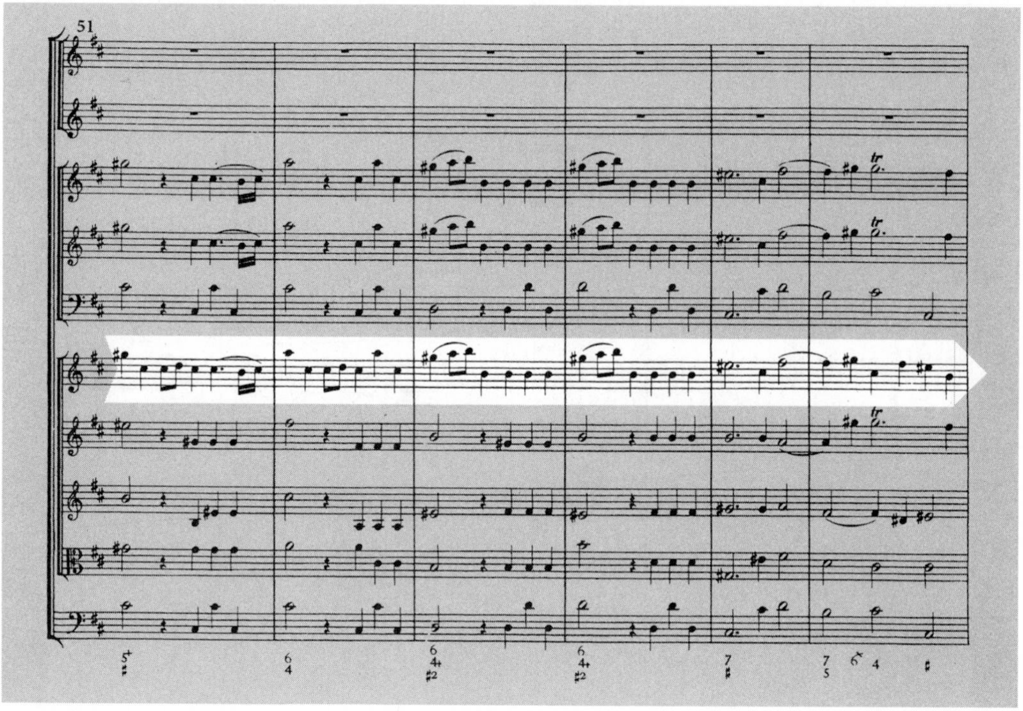
51

The two orchestral suites by George Frideric Handel (1685–1759) are festive pieces intended for outdoor performance. Indeed, *Water Music* (1717) may have been performed on the Thames River, with the musicians on barges providing entertainment for a royal party. The music is unusual in several respects. The traditional order of the suite is abandoned, the continuo part is omitted, and many of the movements, including the two featured in this anthology, avoid the pervasive binary form found in the standard dance suite.

In the Allegro, a series of thematic ideas, extending from two notes to four measures in length, is presented with alternating timbres. The trumpets, accompanied by unison violins, violas, and oboes, initiate the thematic ideas; the horns, accompanied by unison cellos, basses, and bassoons, repeat the material in a lower register. Ultimately, the two groups join forces (m. 38) when the opening phrase returns. In this recording with period instruments, the sound of the valveless brass instruments is striking. Because of their dependency on the natural series of overtones, the brass instruments can only play conjunct melodic material in their higher registers. In keeping with performance practices, a timpani part has been added as a bass for the trumpet family, and during the three-measure transition (Adagio) that separates the two movements, a violinist links the chords with an improvised cadenza.

The hornpipe, set in the standard 3/2 meter associated with the dance, has a ternary (**A-B-A**) form. The **B** section provides a strong contrast by moving from the tonic to B minor. This section features an extended eighth-note passage played by the first violin section that is particularly effective with period instruments. Although this material is new, the accompaniment, with its three quarter-note pick-ups, links the middle section to the second thematic idea of the **A** section.

22. George Frideric Handel

Messiah, excerpts
(1742)

8CD: 2/ 7 – 18
4CD: 1/ 39 – 44

—French Overture Style (Grave, allegro)
—dotted rhythms.

Overture

→ Jennens—librettist (also wrote Saul)
→ 3 parts → 1 + 2 (Christ's life on earth)
→ 3 (reflective)

Editor's note: This edition shows the *Grave* as notated (with simple dotted rhythms) and as played following the Baroque performance practice of rhythmic alteration (resulting in double dotted rhythms). The indication of Sets A and B in the oboe parts refer to variant manuscript sources.

Italian
style
— immitative

✸ Except where specifically marked 'violoncello' by the composer, passages in the *basso continuo* written in the C clefs are treated in this edition as *bassetti* and are not included in the bassoon and cello-bass orchestral parts, unless specially noted, as here.

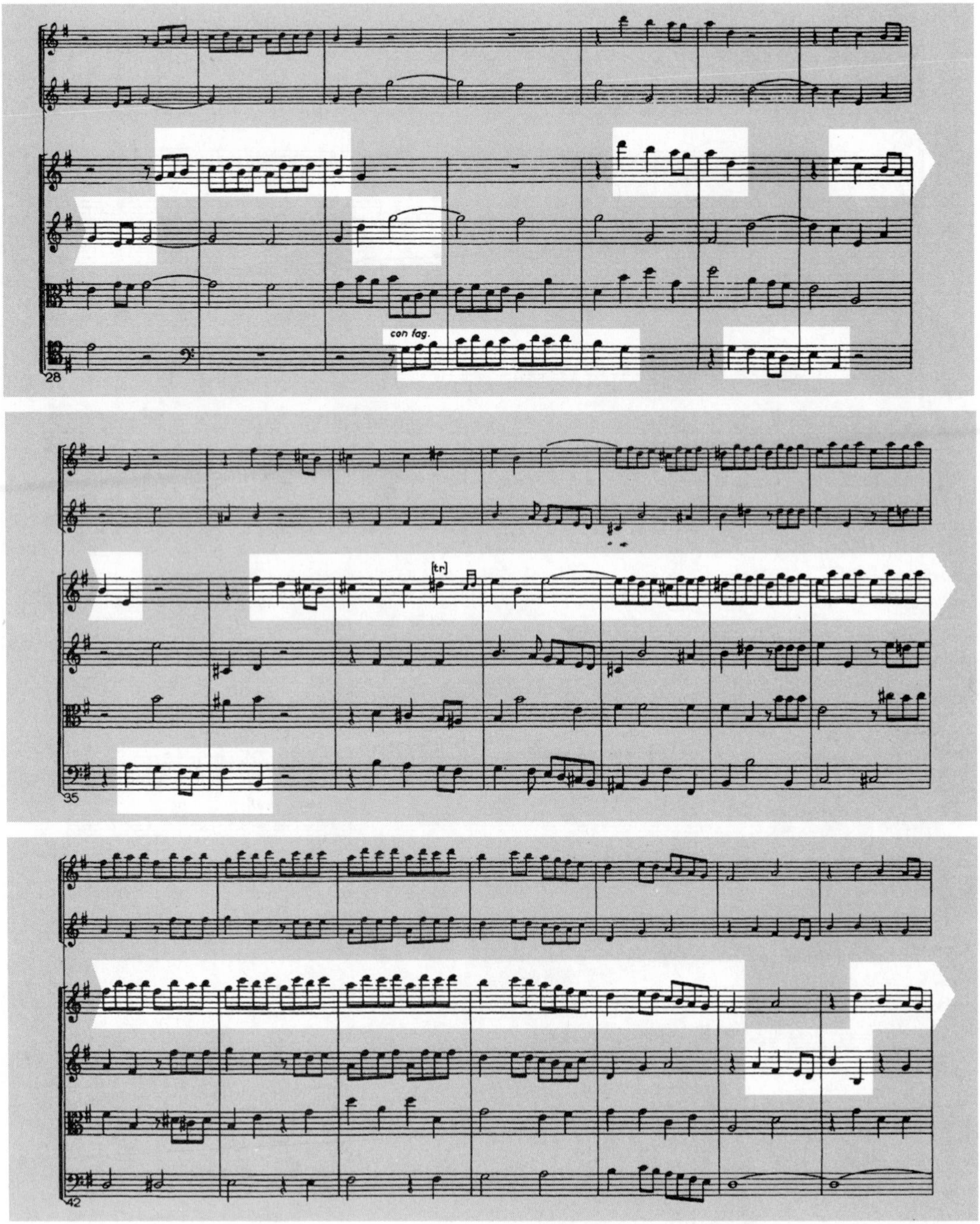
con fag.
28
[tr]
35
42

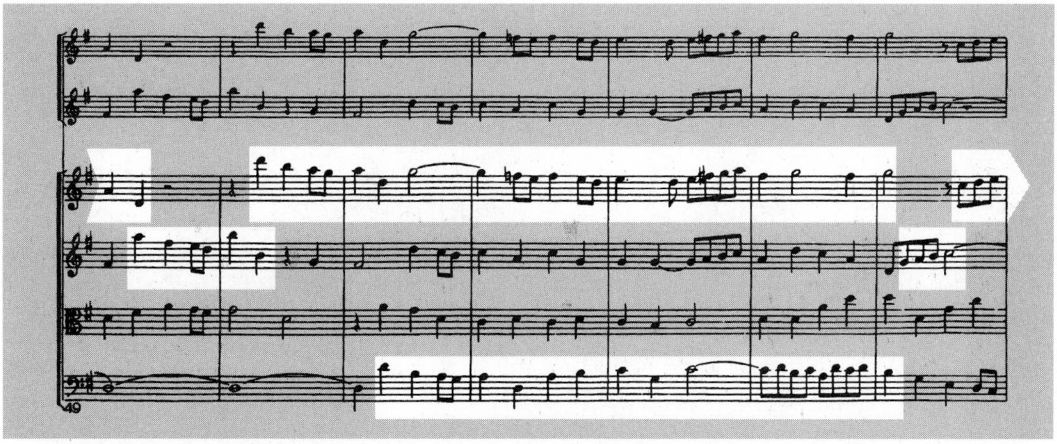
49

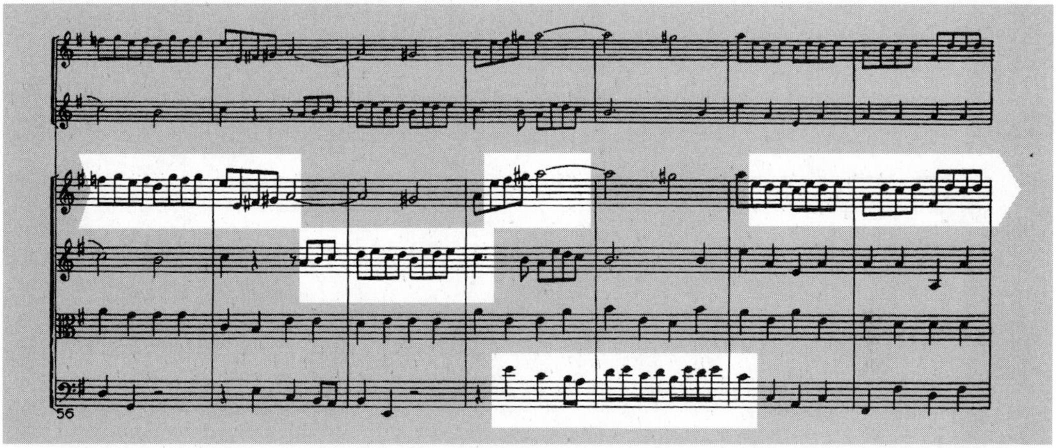
56

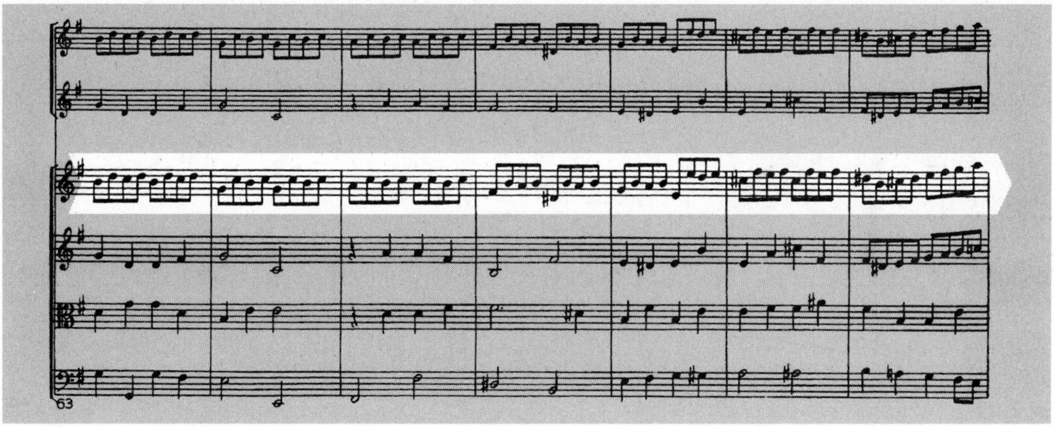
63

22. Handel, *Messiah*: Recitative, "There were shepherds"

No. 14a   Recitative *(secco)*:   THERE WERE SHEPHERDS ABIDING IN THE FIELD

Luke ii, 8

No. 14b   Recitative *(accompagnato)*:   AND, LO, THE ANGEL OF THE LORD CAME UPON THEM

Luke ii, 9

No. 15   Recitative *(secco)*:   AND THE ANGEL SAID UNTO THEM

Luke ii, 10–11

No. 16   Recitative *(accompagnato)*:   AND SUDDENLY THERE WAS WITH THE ANGEL

Luke ii, 13

No. 17   Chorus: GLORY TO GOD
Luke ii, 14

22. Handel, *Messiah*: Chorus, "Glory to God"

Form: A B A (last A shortened)

No. 18
Zechariah ix, 9–10

Aria: REJOICE GREATLY, O DAUGHTER OF ZION

D.C
Aria
→ not
strict

ritornello 1

A

SOPRANO

Re-joice, re-joice, re-joice_____ great-ly, re-joice,_____

O daugh-ter of Zi - on,

madrigal like

O daugh-ter of_ Zi-on, re-joice,_____ re-joice,_____

Editor's note: Tempo, dynamic markings, trills, and other performance markings in
square brackets are editorial. Alternate rhythms reflecting the Baroque performance
practice of rhythmic alteration appear above the music.

153

— english Anthem style (ceremonial)

Chorus: "HALLELUJAH"

No. 44

Rev. xix, 6; xi, 15; xix, 16

16 42

2nd Chorus (chordal A)

Editor's note: Square brackets are used in the accompaniment to show the end of a
passage for a particular instrument or instruments; text is set in capital letters where it
was lacking or abbreviated in the original source.

22. Handel, *Messiah*: Chorus, "Hallelujah"

160

chorale in D+

fugal motif

162

Antiphonal /chordal

(English Anthem)

22. Handel, *Messiah*: Chorus, "Hallelujah"

* Alto: Handel himself wrote both notes.

A returnst Closes

Handel's oratorio *Messiah* (1742) can be seen as a mixture of the Baroque Italian operatic style and the English choral tradition. The overture, however, is fashioned after the model created by Jean-Baptiste Lully in France, commonly known as the French overture. Set in a rounded binary form, the slow tempo, minor key, and dotted rhythms of the opening section create a stately, somber character. The second half of the overture, set in a quicker tempo, features a fugal texture and never strays too far from the home key of E minor. In a performance tradition of French overtures known as overdotting, the dotted rhythms in the slower tempo are altered, so that the dotted quarter notes are lengthened and the eighth notes are shortened.

The Italian opera style can best be heard in the sections for solo voices. Following the Italian tradition, recitatives and arias are clearly separated. The predominant *secco* style of Italian recitative can be heard at the beginning of numbers 14a(⑨) and 15(⑩), and both are followed by *recitative accompagnato* passages in which the texts refer to images of angels. The soprano aria "Rejoice greatly, O daughter of Zion" reflects the Italian predilection for virtuosity and ornamentation, especially in the setting of the word "rejoice." The **A-B-A'** form suggests a *da capo* structure, but the opening **A** section closes in the dominant rather than the tonic, thereby negating the possibility of a literal *da capo* repeat, and the reprise of **A** is truncated.

Handel's mastery of the choral style is clearly evident in the contrasting movements "Glory to God" and the "Hallelujah Chorus." "Glory to God" is a succinct and energetic setting in which the music vividly supports the meaning of the text. In the "Hallelujah Chorus," Handel manipulates a variety of textures to build dramatic tension. At the beginning, he juxtaposes a chordal setting of the word "Hallelujah!" with the monophonic phrase "for the Lord God omnipotent reigneth," and then combines the two in excited counterpoint. The climax of the chorus occurs with the intoning of "King of Kings," punctuated with trumpet, timpani, and the full orchestra.

23. Johann Sebastian Bach
Chorale Prelude, *Ein feste Burg ist unser Gott*
(*A Mighty Fortress Is Our God*) (1709)

8CD: 2/ 19 – 26

Chorale tune

phrase 1

Ein fe - ste Burg _ ist un - ser Gott, ein' gu - te Wehr und _ Waf - fen;
er hilft uns frei _ aus al - ler Not, die uns jetzt hat be - trof - fen.

Der al - te bö - se Feind, mit Ernst er's jetzt meint, gross Macht und viel

List sein grau - sam Rü - stung ist; auf Erd' ist nicht seins - gleich - en.

Editor's note: For translation of chorale text, see p. 258.

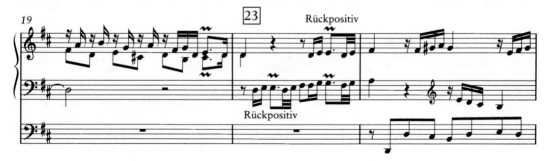

Oberwerk

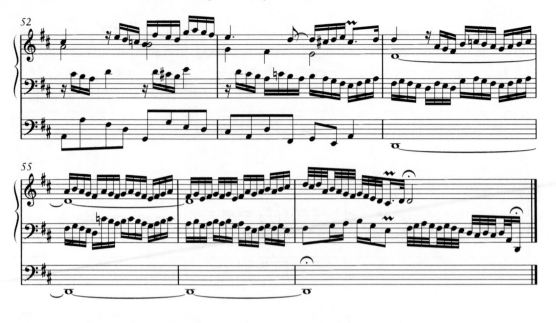

This setting of the famous Lutheran melody *Ein feste Burg ist unser Gott* (*A Mighty Fortress Is Our God*), by J. S. Bach (1685–1750), dates from the composer's Weimar period (1709). Bach composed the prelude for performance on an organ with three keyboards and pedals. By manipulating "stops" that control the airflow into pipes, a performer can create a wide variety of registrations through the isolation and combination of distinct colors, as indicated in the score.

The original chorale, which is attributed to Martin Luther, is in bar form (**A-A-B**). Bach subdivides the melody into nine short phrases. Rather than presenting one consistent approach to the setting of these phrases, as found in most of Bach's later chorale preludes, Bach provides a variety of treatments. For phrases six and seven (mm. 24–33), the tune is intoned in the bass in a cantus firmus fashion, while the upper two voices move in imitation with rapid figurations. The last phrase of the chorale (mm. 40–47) is cast in a similar manner, but with the tune in the highest voice. The other phrases receive varying treatments. In some passages, the tune is clearly heard with only moderate ornamentation (mm. 8–14), and in others, the phrases are obscured by extensive embellishments and imitation. The prelude closes with a coda in which imitation and melodic elaborations on the final phrase push the work to a cadential flourish.

24. Johann Sebastian Bach
Brandenburg Concerto No. 2 in F major,
First and Second Movements (1717–18)

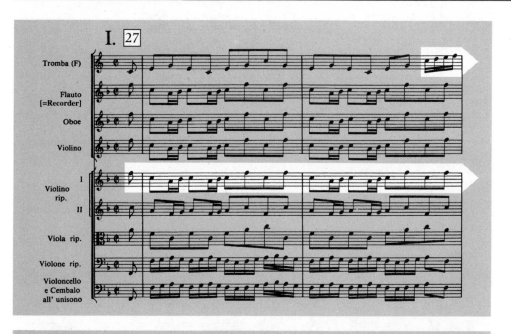

The second of Bach's six concertos dedicated to the margrave of Brandenburg (1717–18) is written for an unusual group of soloists (*concertino*)—violin, oboe, recorder, and trumpet—and a *tutti* string orchestra (*ripieno*) that includes the basso continuo. Although the work maintains ties to the traditions of the concerto grosso, it also exhibits the virtuosity and structure of the solo concerto, including its three-movement format.

As in a Vivaldi solo concerto, the first movement is in ritornello form, and the *tutti* statements help define tonal areas in the closely related major and minor keys. But the prominence of the orchestra during the solo sections and the frequent contrapuntal texture create a more complicated structure than that found in Vivaldi's works. The chamber-music conception of the slow movement provides a strong contrast to the outer movements. The orchestra and trumpet are silent, and the violin, oboe, and recorder play in counterpoint over a walking bass line. All of the thematic material of the movement is derived from the first three measures of the violin solo. The sighing gesture first heard at the end of the initial violin phrase is particularly prominent.

25. Johann Sebastian Bach

Prelude and Fugue in C minor, from
The Well-Tempered Clavier, Book I (1722)

New tuning systems appeared during the Baroque era. Previously, tuning had been based on perfect intervals, which, due to a mathematical quirk of nature, eventually led to increasingly out-of-tune intervals in the circle of fifths. In the seventeenth century, new tuning systems known as equal temperament were explored. By slightly altering the perfect fifth, easier access was gained to all keys. Although the exact nature of Bach's tuning is uncertain, he highlighted the advantage of the newer systems by publishing two sets of preludes and fugues in each of the twenty-four major and minor keys (forty-eight works in all) entitled *The Well-Tempered Clavier.*

Bach completed the first of the two sets in 1722. The Prelude in C minor contains two melodic lines, similar to a two-part invention. For the most part, each line contains a steady stream of sixteenth notes that outline a single harmony for every measure. Following the dissonant minor ninth interval in measure 24, the prelude launches into a freer, cadenza-like passage that brings the perpetual motion to a close. The following three-voice fugue follows a standard fugal format. It begins with three statements of the theme in the exposition. Subsequent entries appear in other keys, but the tonic returns near the end featuring a few last thematic statements.

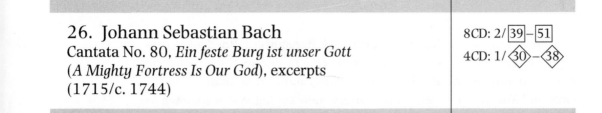

26. Johann Sebastian Bach

Cantata No. 80, *Ein feste Burg ist unser Gott*
(*A Mighty Fortress Is Our God*), excerpts
(1715/c. 1744)

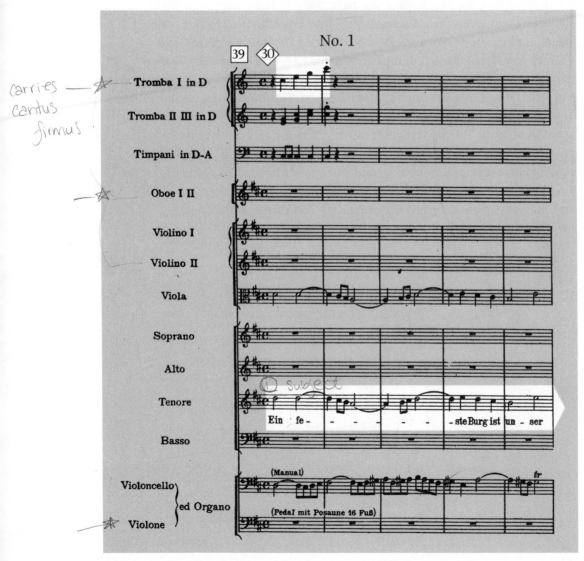

Editor's note: For original version of chorale tune, see p. 170. Trumpets and timpani
were added by Wilhelm Friedemann Bach.

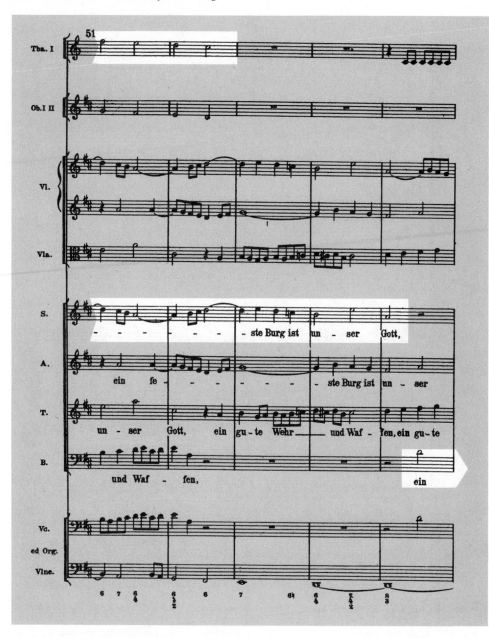

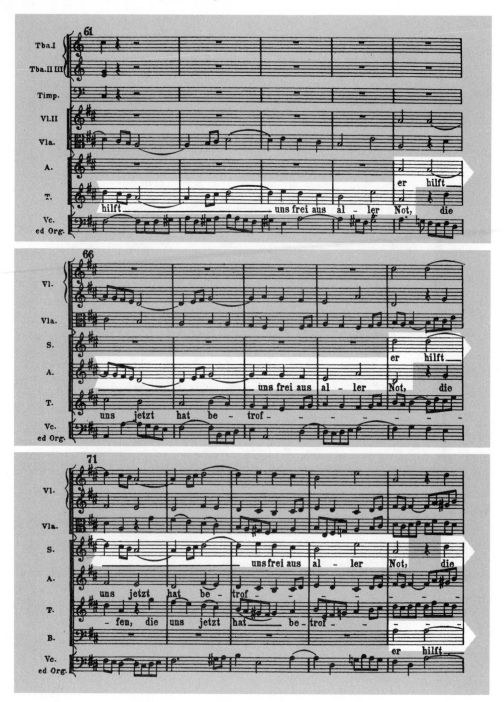

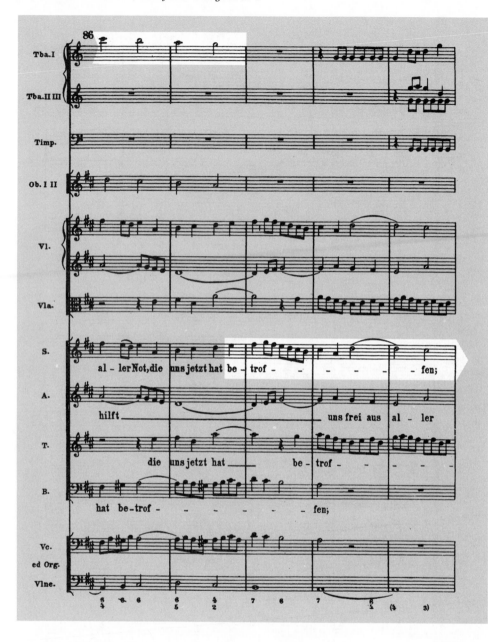

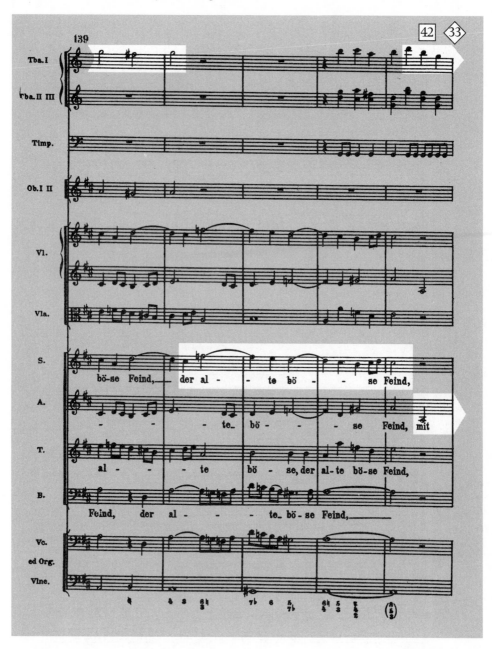

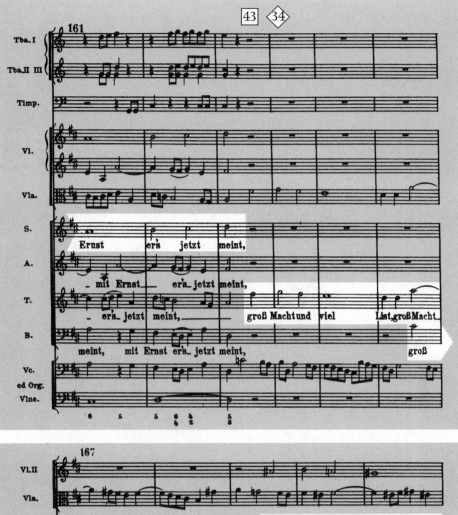

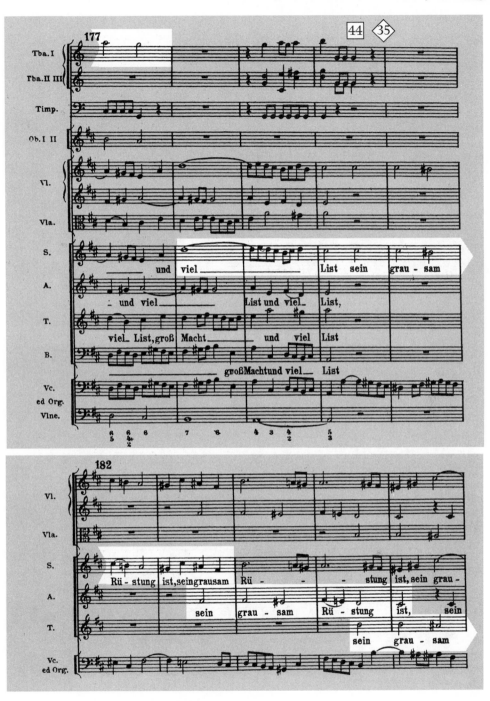

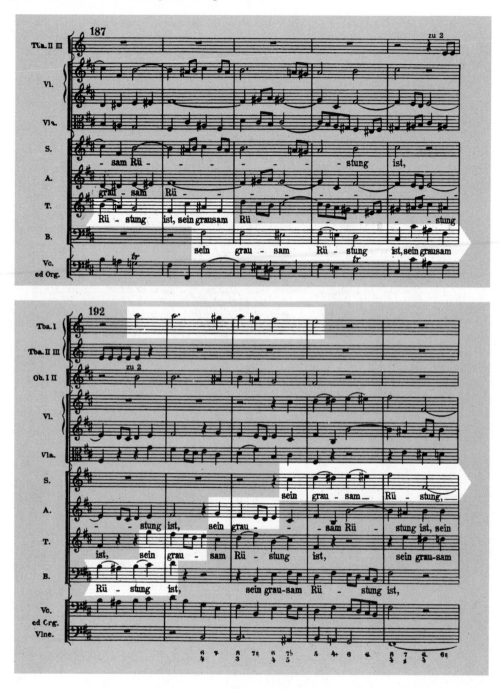

18
Ob.
Vl. e Vla.
S.
ren.
B.
ren, ist zum Sie-gen aus-er-ko - - - - - - -
Cont.
20
Vl. e Vla.
B.
- - - - - - - - - - ren, zum Sie-gen
Cont.
23
Ob.
Vl. e Vla.
S.
Es streit für uns ___ der rech -
B.
aus - erko - ren. Al - - les, al - - -
Cont.
26
Ob.
tr
Vl. e Vla.
S.
tr
- - te, der rech - te Mann,
B.
- - les, was von Gott ge - bo - ren, al - les, was von Gott ge -
Cont.

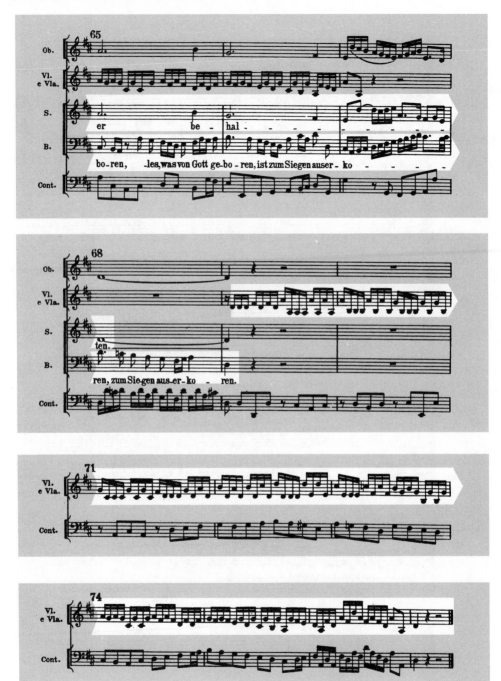

No. 5

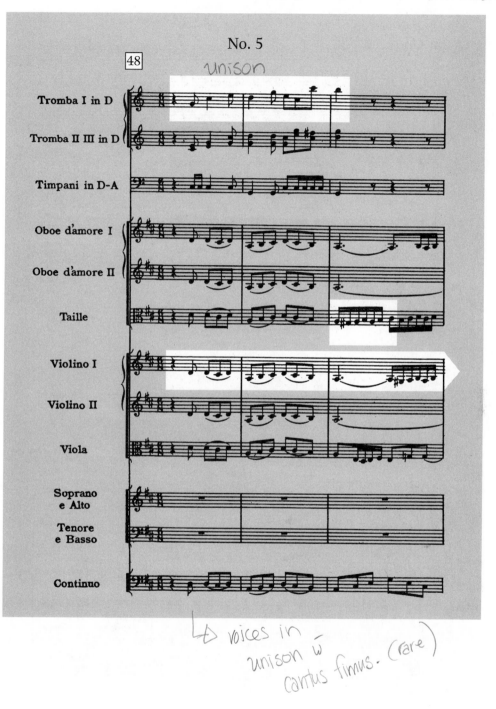

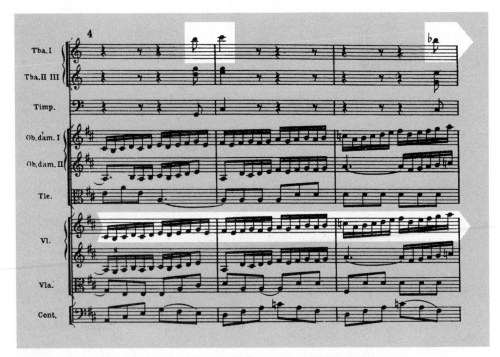

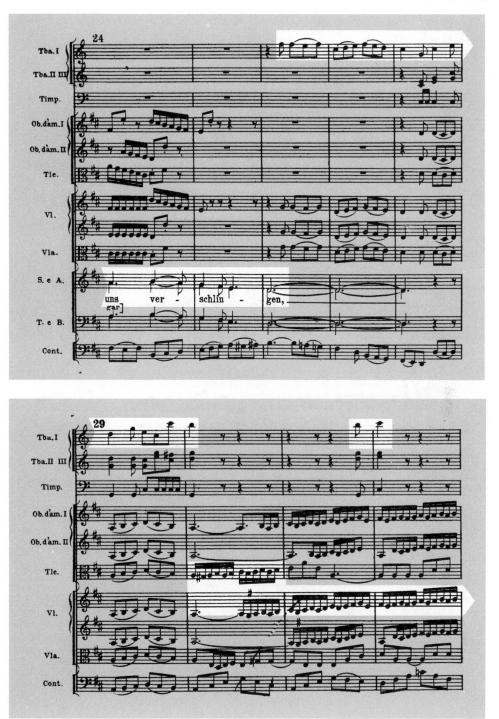

39
Tba I
Tba. II III
Timp.
Ob.d'am. I
Ob.d'am. II
Tle.
Vl.
Vla.
S. e A.
so fürch - ten wir uns
T. e B.
Cont.

43
Tba. I
Tba. II III
Ob.d'am. I
Ob.d'am. II
Tle.
Vl.
Vla.
S. e A.
nicht so sehr,
T. e B.
Cont.

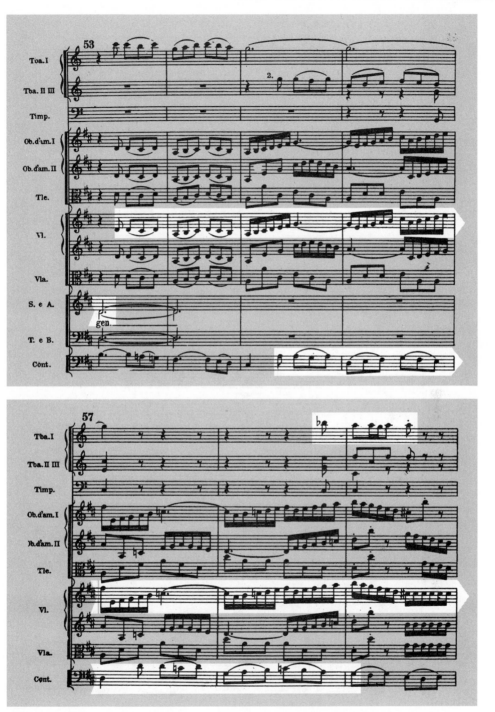

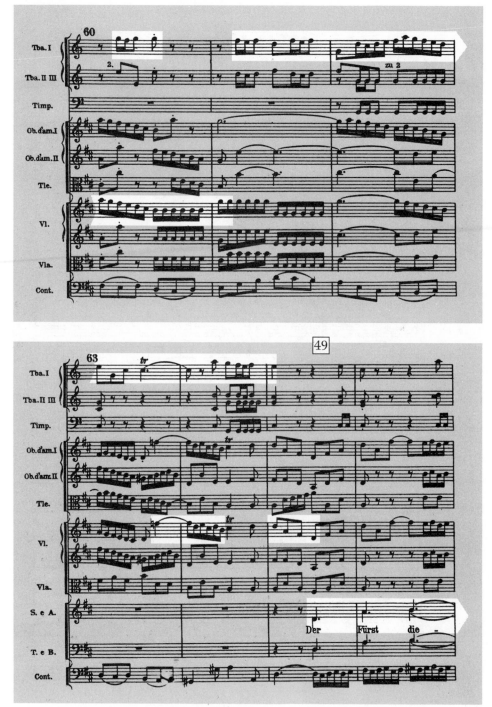

chromatic because talking about devil.

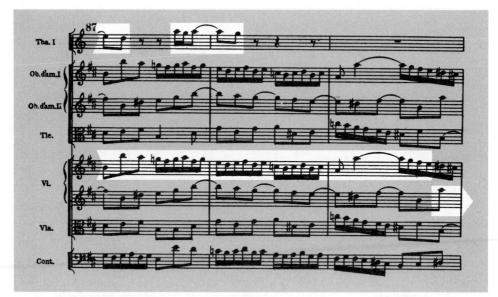

106
Tba. I
Tba. II III
Timp.
Ob.d'am. I
Ob.d'am. II
Tle.
Vl.
Vla.
S. e A.
T. e B.
Cont.

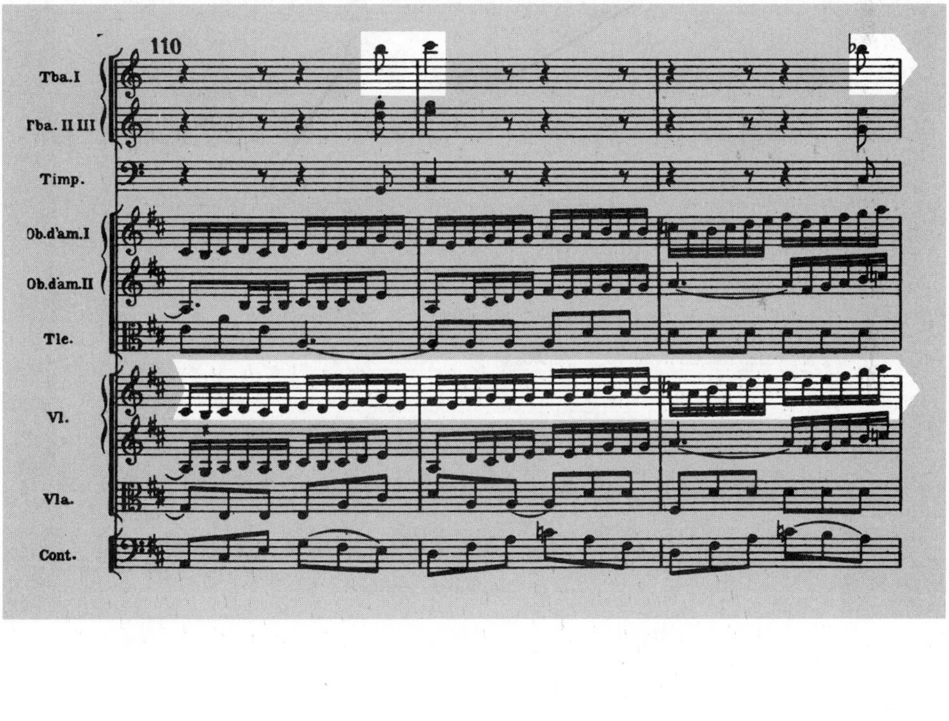
110
Tba. I
Tba. II III
Timp.
Ob.d'am. I
Ob.d'am. II
Tle.
Vl.
Vla.
Cont.

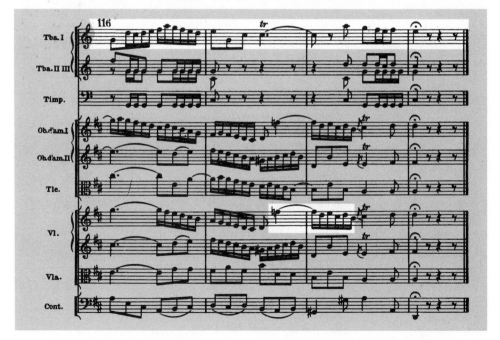

26. Bach, Cantata No. 80, *Ein feste Burg*

Text and Translation

1. Choral Fugue

Ein feste Burg ist unser Gott,
ein' gute Wehr und Waffen;
er hilft uns frei aus aller Not,
die uns jetzt hat betroffen

Der alte böse Feind,
mit Ernst er's jetzt meint,
gross Macht und viel List;
sein grausam Rüstung ist;
auf Erd' ist nicht seinsgleichen.

A mighty fortress is our God,
a good defense and weapon;
He helps free us from all the troubles
that have now befallen us.

Our ever evil foe,
in earnest plots against us,
with great strength and cunning
he prepares his dreadful plans.
Earth holds none like him.

2. Duet
Soprano

Mit unser Macht ist nichts getan,
wir sind gar bald verloren.
Es streit't für uns der rechte Mann,
den Gott selbst hat erkoren.

Fragst du, wer er ist?
Er heisst Jesus Christ,
der Herre Zebaoth,
und ist kein andrer Gott,
das Feld muss er behalten.

With our own strength nothing is achieved.
we would soon be lost.
But on our behalf strives the Mighty One,
whom God Himself has chosen.

Ask you, who is he?
He is called Jesus Christ,
Lord of Hosts,
And there is no other God,
He must remain master of the field.

Bass

Alles was von Gott geboren,
ist zum Siegen auserkoren.
Wer bei Christi Blutpanier
in der Taufe Treu' geschworen,
siegt im Geiste für und für.

Everything born of God
has been chosen for victory.
He who holds to Christ's banner,
truly sworn in baptism,
his spirit will conquer forever and ever.

5. Chorus

Und wenn die Welt voll Teufel wär
und wollten uns verschlingen,
so fürchten wir uns nicht so sehr,
es soll uns doch gelingen.

Der Fürst dieser Welt,
wie saur er sich stellt,
tut er uns doch nicht,
das macht, er ist gericht't,
ein Wörtlein kann ihn fällen.

Though the world were full of devils
eager to devour us,
we need have no fear,
as we will still prevail.

The arch-fiend of this world,
no matter how bitter his stand,
cannot harm us,
indeed he faces judgment,
one Word from God will bring him low.

8. Chorale

Das Wort sie sollen lassen stahn	Now let the Word of God abide
und kein Dank dazu haben.	without further thought.
Er ist bei uns wohl auf dem Plan	He is firmly on our side
mit seinem Geist und Gaben.	with His spirit and strength.
Nehmen sie uns den Leib,	Though they deprive us of life,
Gut, Ehr', Kind, und Weib,	wealth, honor, child, and wife,
lass fahren dahin,	we will not complain,
sie haben's kein Gewinn;	it will avail them nothing;
das Reich muss uns doch bleiben.	for God's kingdom must prevail.

In his positions with several Lutheran churches, and particularly as cantor of St. Thomas's in Leipzig, Bach composed over two-hundred cantatas. His cantata *Ein feste Burg ist unser Gott* (*A Mighty Fortress Is Our God*) was originally written in Weimar for performance during Lent. Since cantatas were not performed during Lent in Leipzig, Bach adapted the cantata for the Feast of the Reformation (October 31), which commemorates the day that Martin Luther posted his ninety-five theses in 1517.

Bach frequently incorporated chorale tunes in his sacred works, and his Cantata No. 80 features the chorale *Ein feste Burg ist unser Gott*, attributed to Martin Luther himself. In its final version, the cantata contains eight movements, and the chorale appears in movements 1, 2, 5, and 8. The other movements are recitatives and arias for solo singers. Typical of Bach, the most elaborate setting of the chorale melody is in the opening movement. Bach retains the original bar form of the tune (**A-A-B**) and subdivides the **A** section into two phrases and the **B** section into five phrases. Each phrase of the chorale tune is heard in the oboes and trumpets. Preceding these statements are choral fugues based on the individual chorale phrases.

The second movement sets the tune in a four-part texture. The accompanying parts consist of a perpetual-motion unison string line, a walking bass line, and a virtuoso solo bass melody. The solo soprano and oboes present an ornamented version of the tune, sometimes in a heterophonic texture. In the fifth movement, a unison choir intones the chorale, while the orchestra plays an elaborate accompaniment. The simplest presentation of the tune is in the final movement, where the entire congregation would have joined in singing the melody. The chorale is set in a simple, homophonic, four-part texture, with the melody in the top voice.

27. John Gay

The Beggar's Opera, end of Act II (1728)

Air 38. "Why how now, Madam Flirt?"
(*Good-morrow, Gossip Joan*)

(To her)
Sau - cy Jade!

CUE: PEACHUM Sure all Women are alike! If ever they commit the Folly, they are sure to commit another by exposing themselves —
Away — Not a word more — You are my Prisoner now, Hussy.

Air 39. "No pow'r on earth"
(*Irish Howl*, by George Vanbrughe)

POLLY No pow'r on earth can e'er di - vide The knot that sac - red Love hath ty'd.

When par - ents draw a - gainst our mind, The true - love's knot they fast - er bind.

(Play text: Oh, oh ray, oh Am - bo - rah oh, oh, &c.)
Ho ho ra in am - bo - ra ho an ho der-ry hi an hi der-ry

CUE: MACHEATH A Moment of time may make us unhappy forever.

Air 40. "I like the Fox shall grieve"
(*The Lass of Patie's Mill*)

Version A

Editor's note: Because of a weak bass part in this piece (given as Version A here), the editor, Jeremy Barlow, prepared an alternative version from another eighteenth-century source (Version B), which is performed on the Norton recording.

With *The Beggar's Opera*, John Gay (1685–1732) established a new tradition for the ballad opera that would enjoy widespread popularity. Following a simple formula, Gay inserted a number of songs into a spoken comedic play. The songs were not original, but were borrowed from a variety of sources, generally popular, with the words changed to meet the needs of the play. For the most part, the tunes are simple, short, and accompanied by basso continuo or small ensemble.

The end of Act II contains three contrasting songs. Air 38 is a delightful strophic duet. Lucy and Polly take turns taunting each other with a twelve-measure tune embellished lightly with operatic flourishes. Air 39, in which Polly sings of her love for Macheath, is a simple **A-A-B-C** tune that reaches its highest point in the last phrase. The close on the dominant suggests the staging, as her father is pulling her away. The act closes with a sentimental melody, Air 40, in which Lucy acknowledges that by helping Macheath, she will never see him again. The binary form of the melody suggests a dance conception for the original tune.

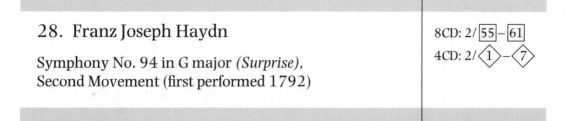

28. Franz Joseph Haydn

Symphony No. 94 in G major *(Surprise)*,
Second Movement (first performed 1792)

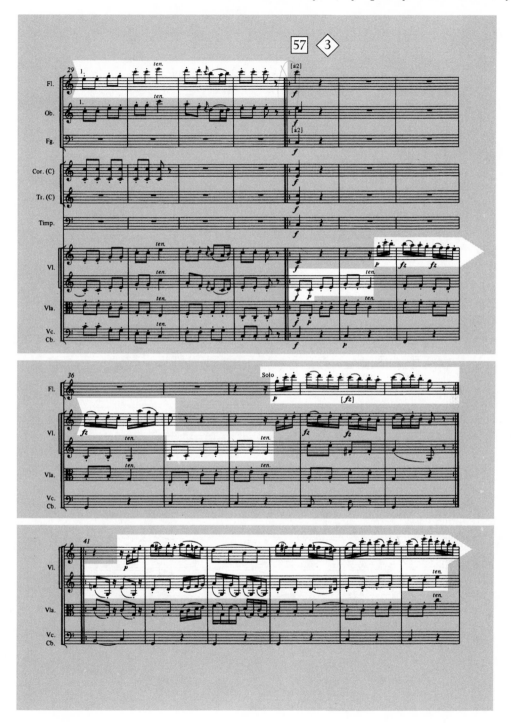

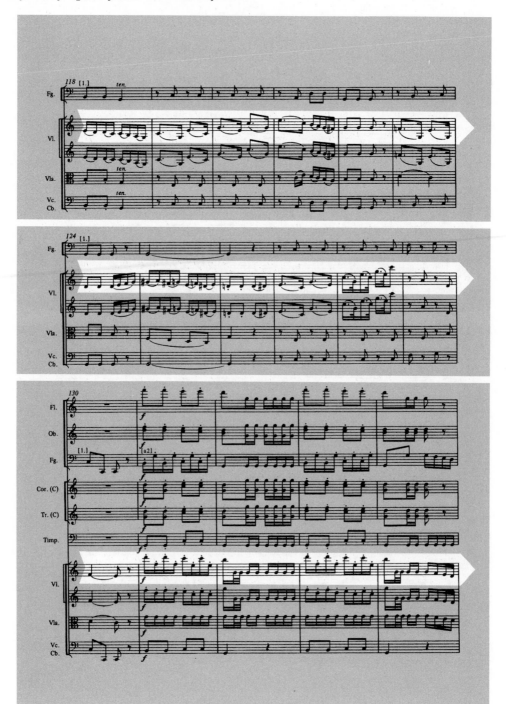

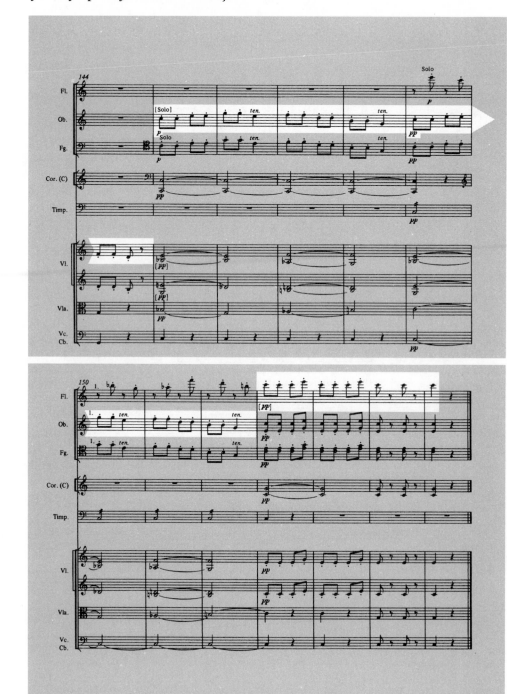

The last twelve symphonies of Franz Joseph Haydn (1732–1809) were written for subscription concerts in London directed by the violinist Johann Peter Salomon. Haydn himself played continuo on a fortepiano during the performances, while Salomon led the orchestra from the concertmaster position. The performance on period instruments in the accompanying recording allows us to hear the timbres and clarity of sound that would have delighted an eighteenth-century audience.

Haydn's Symphony No. 94 is clearly the most popular work of the *London* Symphonies. The work derives its nickname from the celebrated "surprise" that occurs in measure 16 of the second movement. The notoriety of this moment is well deserved, as it typifies Haydn's keen sense of wit and humor. The surprise is set up by the presentation of a quiet, simple melodic phrase, its repetition at an even softer dynamic level, and the placement of the jolt on the weak beat of the measure. The joke is made even more pronounced, as the orchestra continues to present the remainder of the rounded binary theme as if nothing had happened.

The simplicity of the theme-and-variations structure allows Haydn to play with the natural expectations of the listener. For the most part, the variations retain the tune and structure as heard in the opening theme. The most striking deviations occur in variations two and four. The second variation, which begins with two sudden harmonic shifts to C minor and E-flat major, launches into an intense developmental passage that replaces the second half of the theme. Variation four presents variations within a variation, as the repetition of each phrase is altered. A coda follows that features fleeting fragments of the tune in the winds, over chromatic harmonies in the strings.

29. Franz Joseph Haydn

String Quartet, Op. 76, No. 2 *(Quinten),*
Fourth Movement (1797)

During the 1790s, the string quartet underwent a transformation from an intimate form of household entertainment to a theatrical concert piece. Elements of both conceptions can be seen in Haydn's late quartets. In the last movement of his String Quartet in D minor, Haydn mixes folk characteristics, virtuosic display, and humor within the framework of the sonata-allegro form. The exposition, written without repeats, presents three principal themes: the first is a binary tune suggesting a Hungarian dance, the second makes a brief appearance, and the closing theme appears over a tonic pedal. The development and recapitulation, in typical Haydn fashion, continue to delight with unexpected turns and flourishes. In the recapitulation, Haydn begins to develop ideas immediately at the close of the first theme, as he mixes various motives together. After a held dominant-seventh chord, the first theme returns quietly in D major, and this key remains through the recapitulation and the brief, theatrical coda.

30. Franz Joseph Haydn

Die Schöpfung (The Creation), Part I, excerpts
(first performed 1799)

No. 12   Recitative (Uriel)

Und Gott sprach: Es sei'n Lichter an der Feste des Himmels · *And God said: Let there be lights in the firmament of heaven*

No. 13   Recitative (Uriel)

In vollem Glanze steiget jetzt die Sonne strahlend auf · *In splendour bright the sun is rising now*

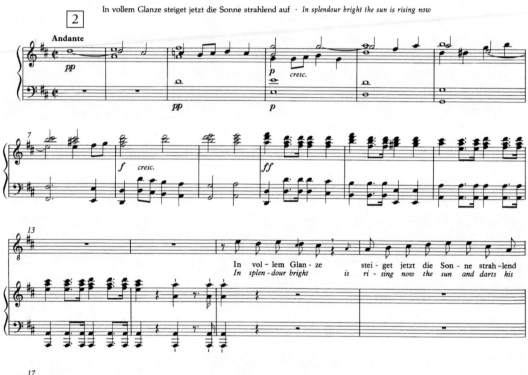

ein Rie - se stolz und froh zu ren - nen sei - ne
a gi - ant proud and glad to run his mea - sur'd

Bahn. Mit lei - sem Gang und sanf - tem Schim - mer
course. With soft - er beams and mild - er light steps on the

schleicht der Mond die stil - le Nacht hin - durch. Den
sil - ver moon thro' si - lent night. The

aus - ge - dehn - ten Him - mels - raum ziert oh - ne Zahl der
space im - mense of th'a - zure sky in - num - 'rous host of

hel - len Ster - ne Gold, und die Söh - ne Got - tes ver - kün - dig - ten den vier - ten
ra - diant orbs a - dorns, and the sons of God an - noun - ced the fourth

No. 14 Chorus and Trio

Die Himmel erzählen die Ehre Gottes · *The heavens are telling the glory of God*

30. Haydn, *Die Schöpfung:* Chorus, "Die Himmel erzählen"

Inspired by performances of Handel's oratorios in London, Haydn composed two oratorios late in his career. The first of these, *Die Schöpfung* (*The Creation*), draws its text from Genesis and Milton's *Paradise Lost*. Part I of the work deals with the first four days of Creation, concluding with two recitatives by Uriel (tenor soloist) and the chorus "Die Himmel erzählen" ("The Heavens Are Telling"). The first recitative is accompanied by the basso continuo *(secco)* and is characterized by a limited range, repeated notes, and a sparse accompaniment. The second recitative, which opens with a stunning orchestral crescendo depicting the rising sun, is accompanied by the orchestra *(accompagnato)*, treats the melodic line more freely, and contains several notable examples of word painting.

"Die Himmel erzählen" alternates three sections for chorus with two passages sung by the trio of angels. The first choral section presents three four-measure phrases **(A-B-B),** which serve as material for the other choral and solo sections. The energy of the movement, which builds from the simple beginning through more complicated textures, climaxes with a fugal passage and a final choral statement accompanied by brass and timpani.

31. Wolfgang Amadeus Mozart

Piano Sonata in A major, K. 331,
Third Movement (1783)

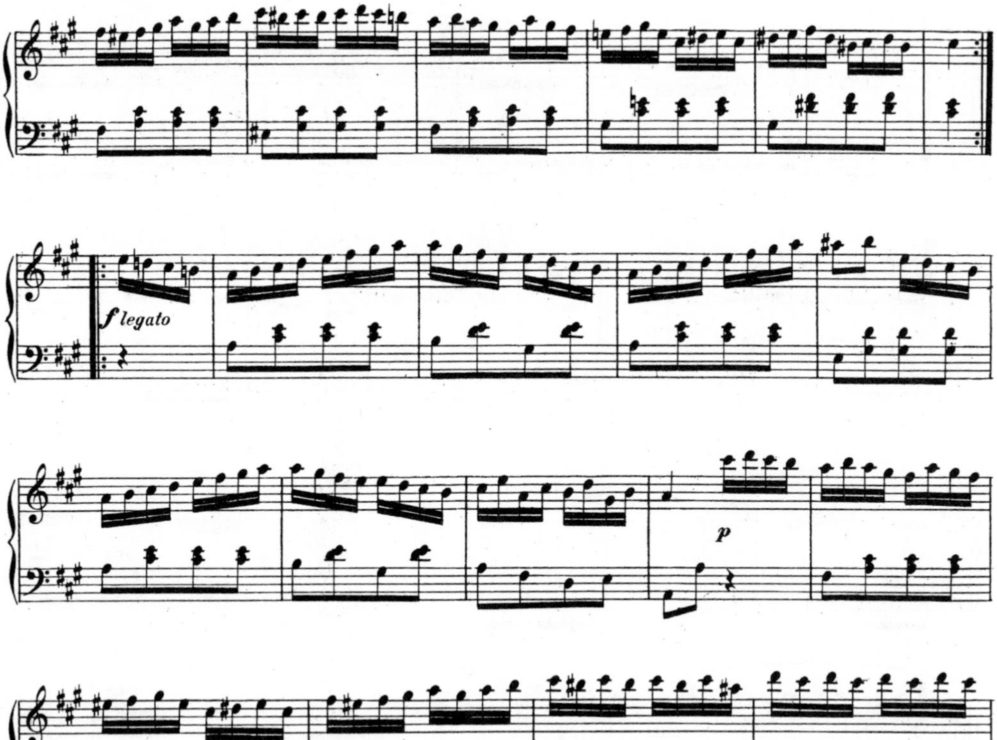
f legato
p
7
f

31. Mozart, Piano Sonata in A major, K. 331: III

The piano sonata became one of the most popular genres of the Classical era. Although the number of movements varies from two to four, the individual movements of a sonata approximate the form and style of their counterparts in a symphony. The rondo finale to the three-movement Piano Sonata in A major, K. 331, by W. A. Mozart (1756–1791), is set in an unusual format: **A-B-C-B-A-B-coda.** The performance with a fortepiano on the recording brings out the different timbres of the registers and provides great clarity both to the sixteenth-note passages and to individual chords.

At the time that this sonata was composed (1783), Vienna was under the spell of the exotic styles and sounds of Turkey. Mozart exploited this fascination with Turkey throughout the movement. The clanging sounds of a Turkish Janissary band can be heard in Mozart's rolled chords, quick ornaments, and drones. Another fascinating Turkish tradition is the whirling dervish ritual, a dance featuring a controlled spinning motion, which is suggested by the continuous whirling sixteenth-note material of sections **A** and **C.**

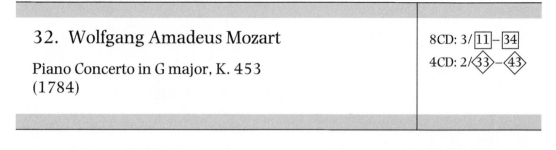

32. Wolfgang Amadeus Mozart

Piano Concerto in G major, K. 453
(1784)

8CD: 3/ 11 – 34
4CD: 2/ 33 – 43

Editor's note: The cadenzas included in this score are Mozart's own.

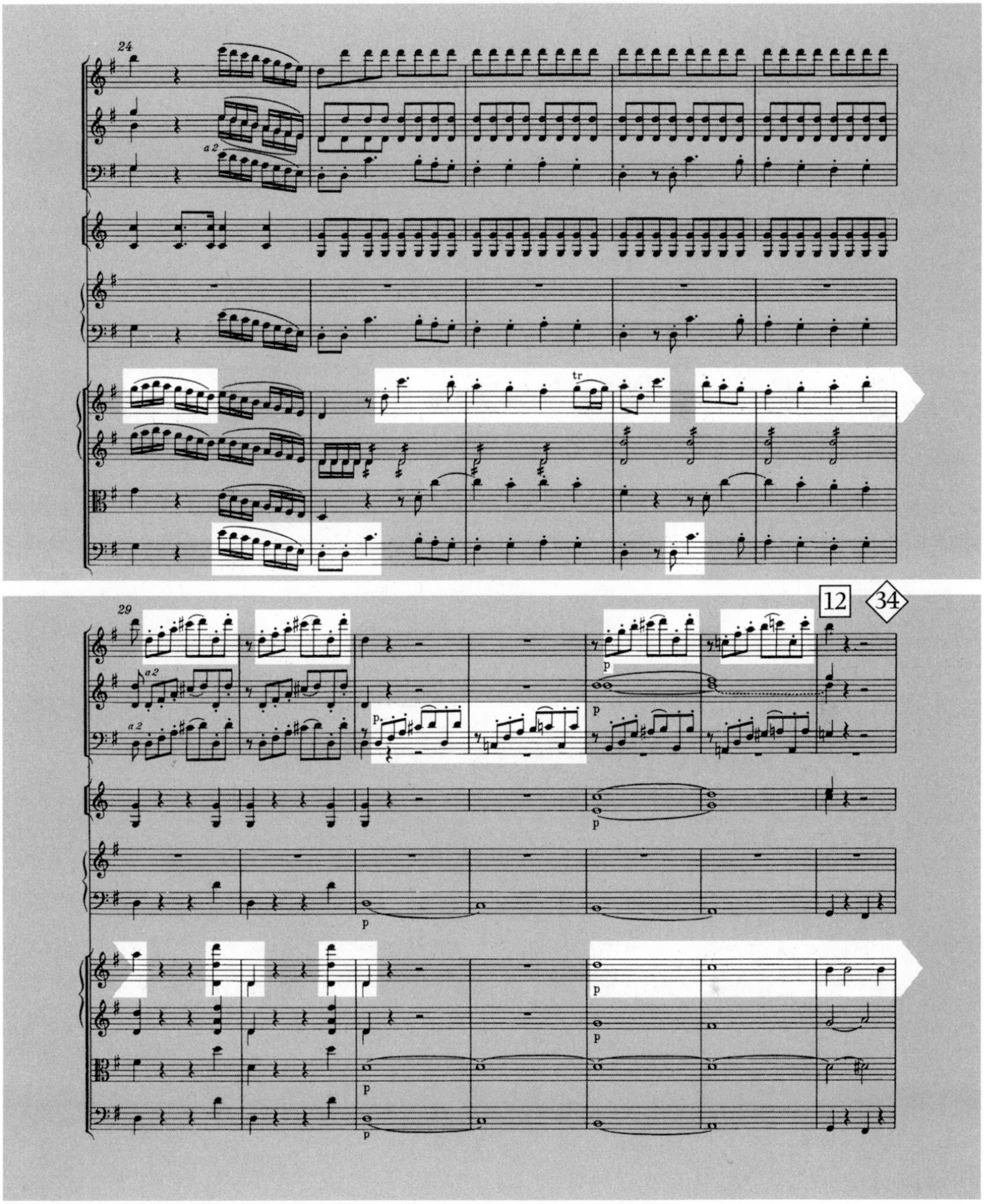
24
a 2
tr
29
a 2
a 2
p
12
34

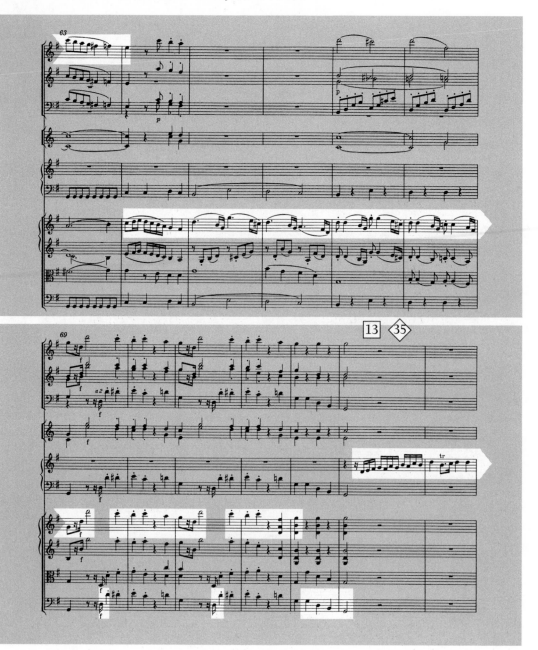

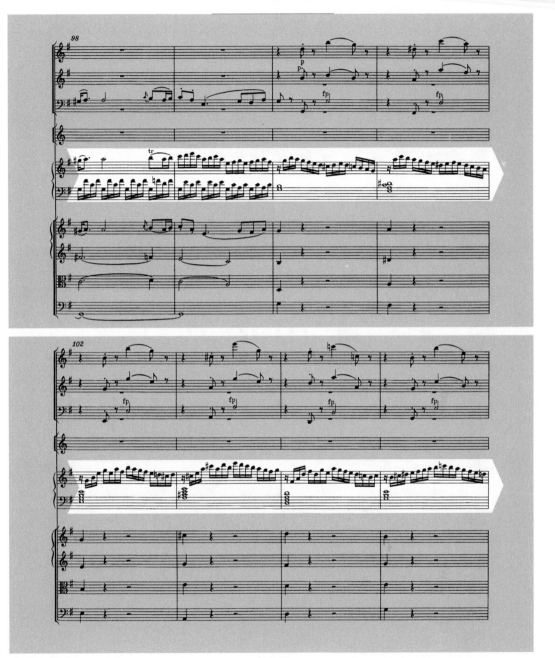

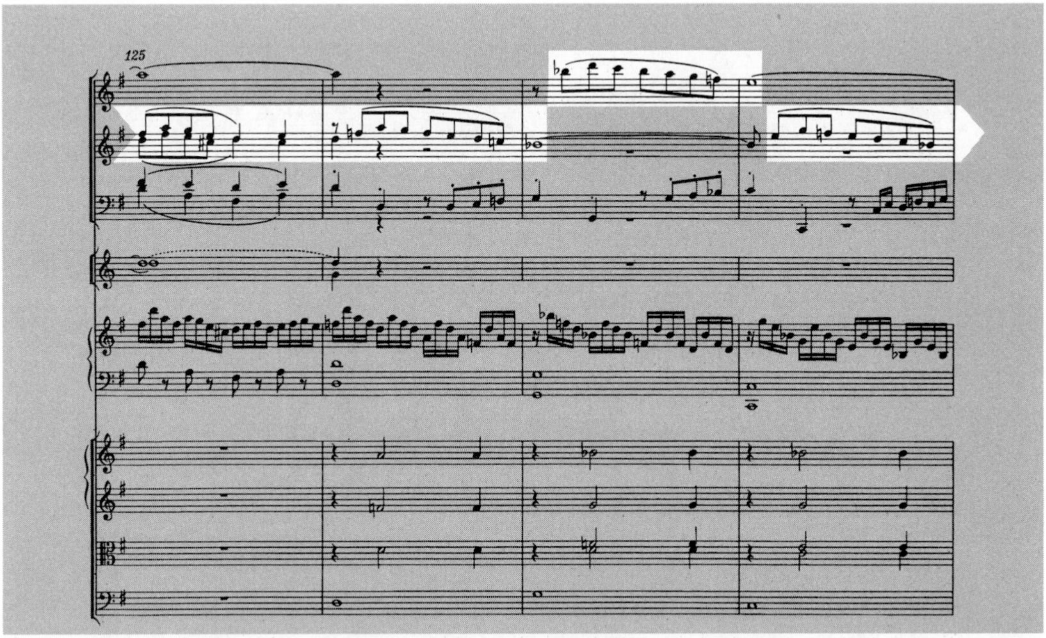
125

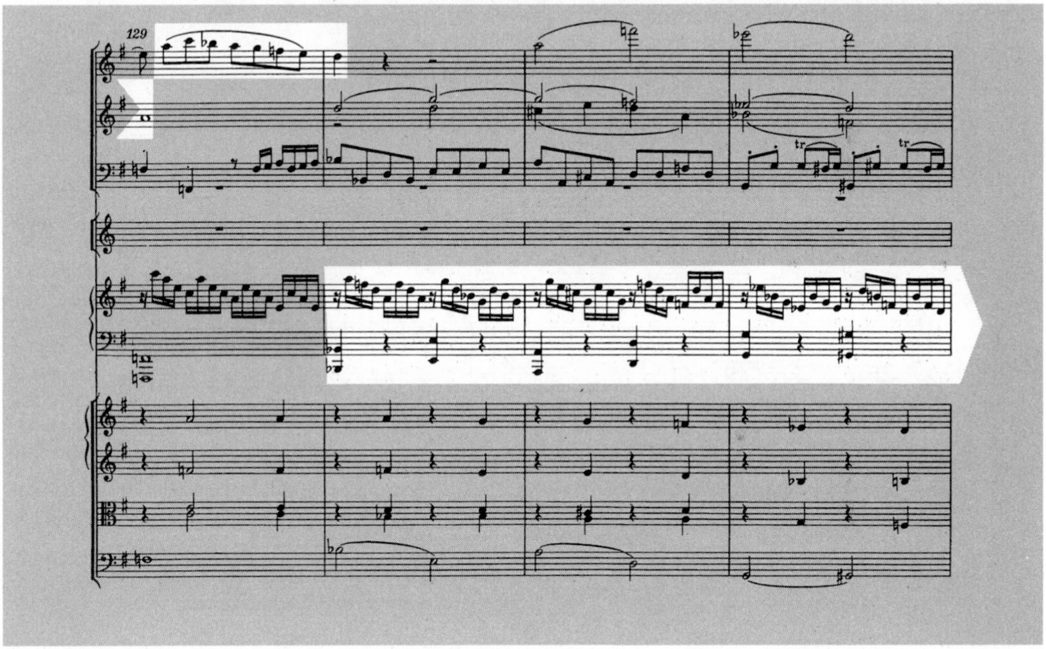
129
tr
tr

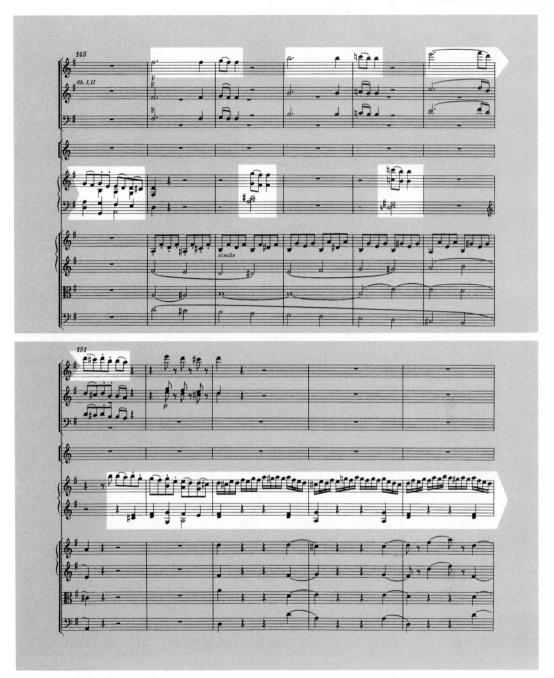

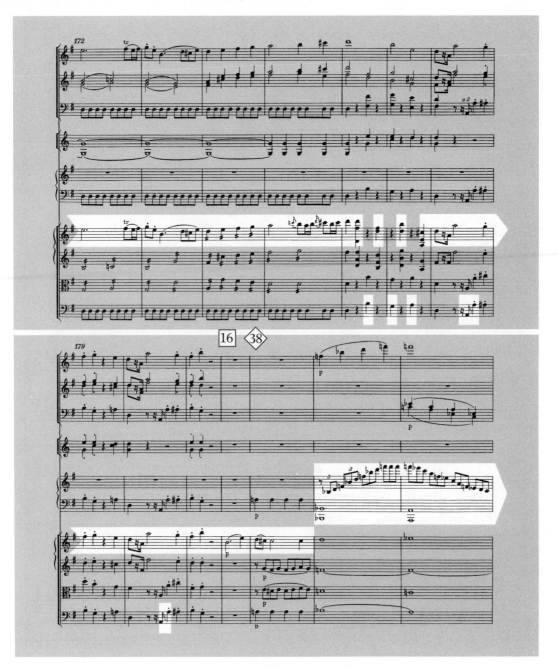

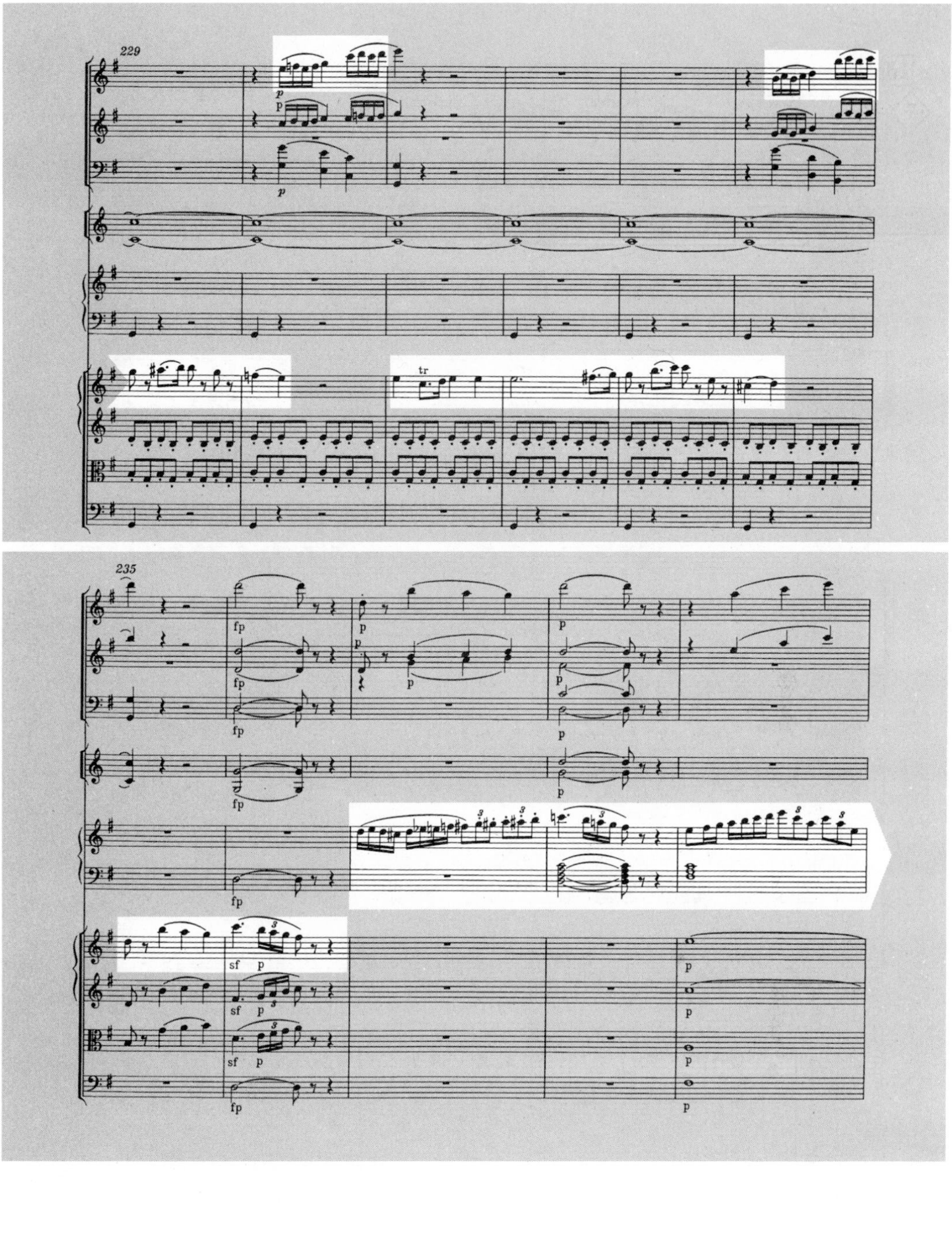
229
235

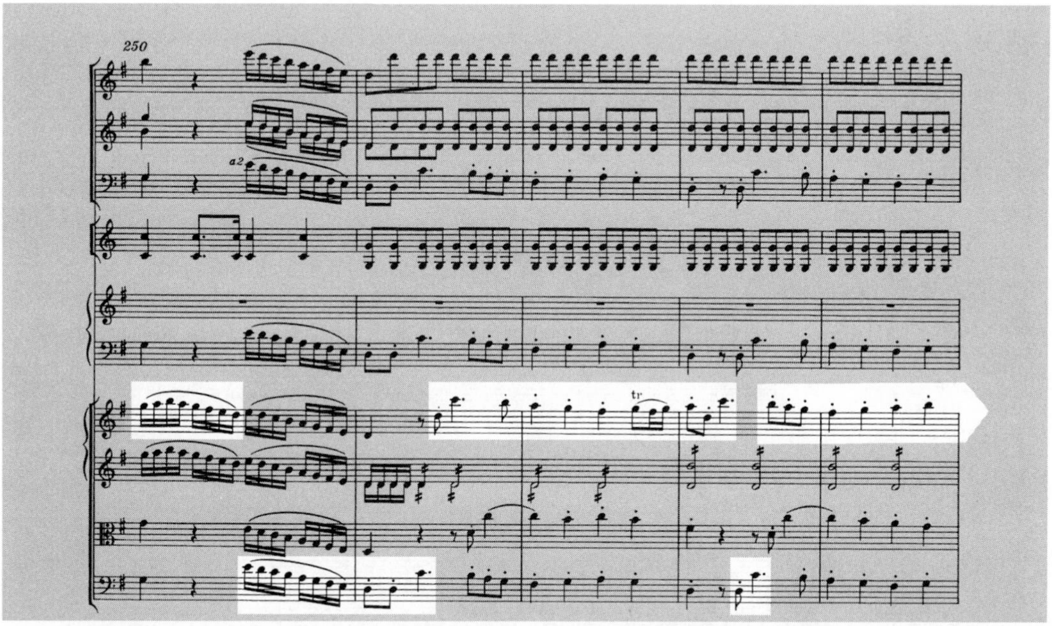
250
a2
tr

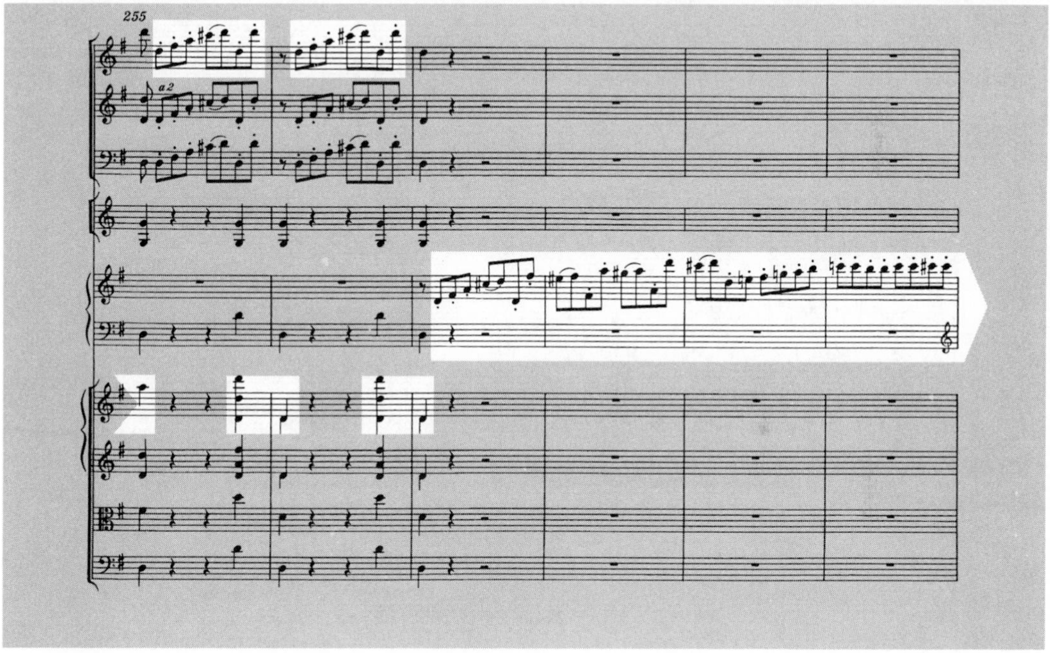
255
a2

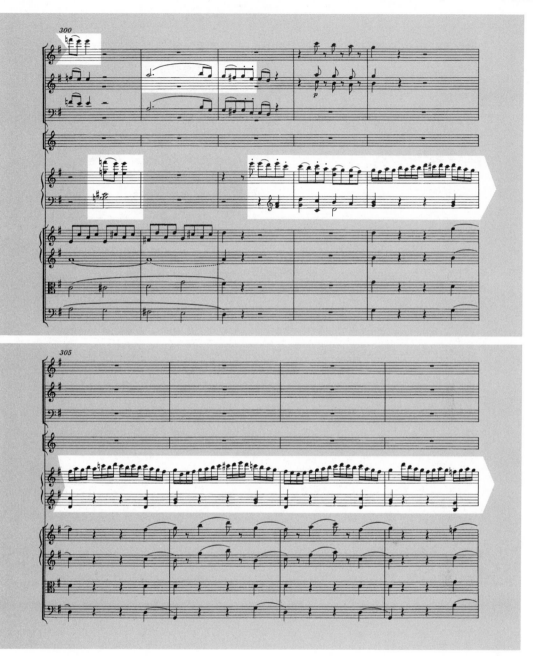

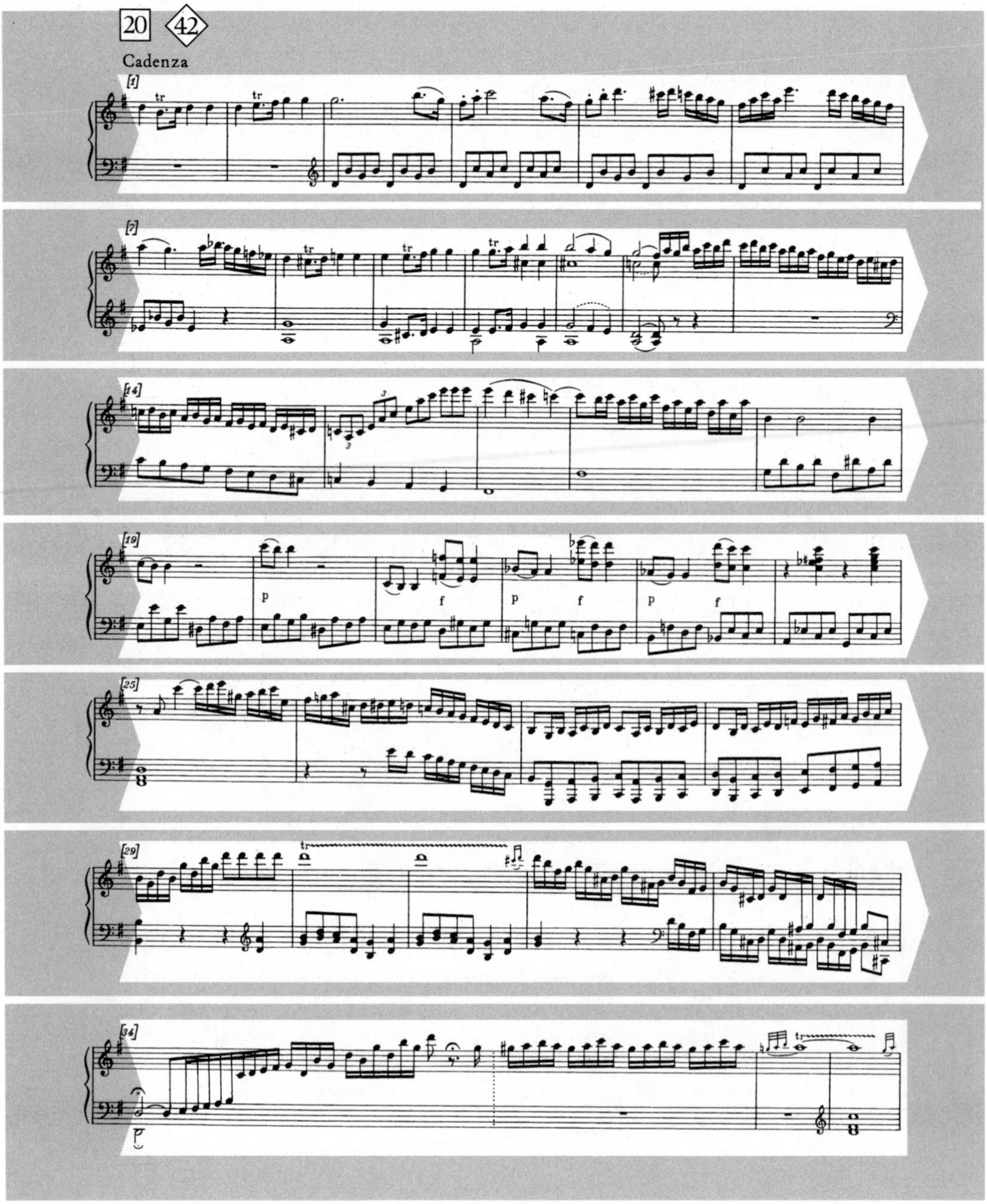
20
42
Cadenza
[1]
tr
[7]
[14]
[19]
p
f
[25]
[29]
[34]

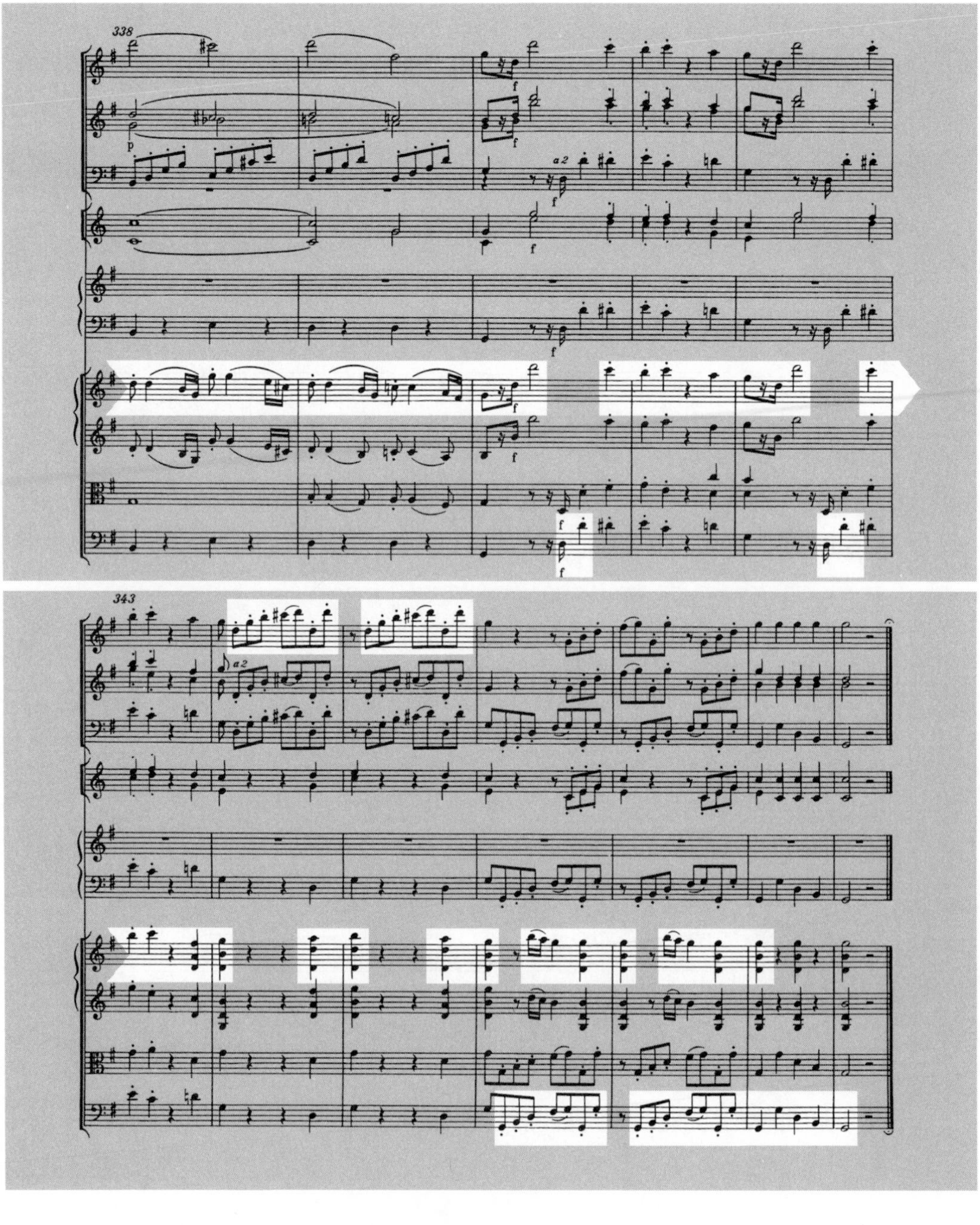
338
a2
343
a2

II

32. Mozart, Piano Concerto in G major, K. 453: II

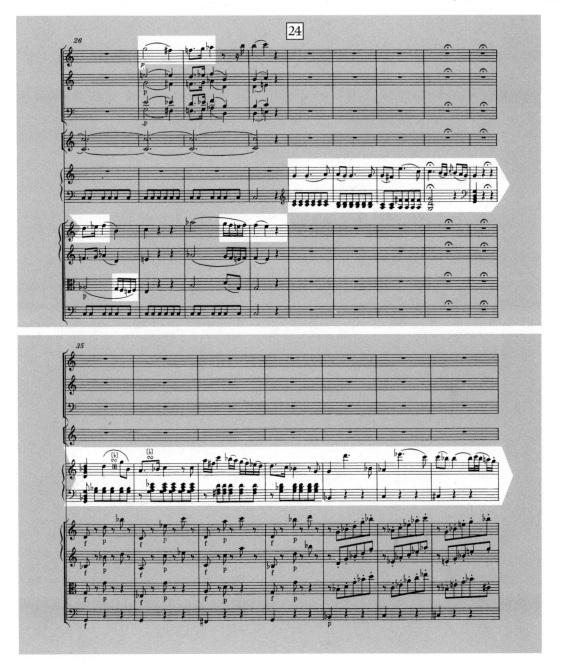

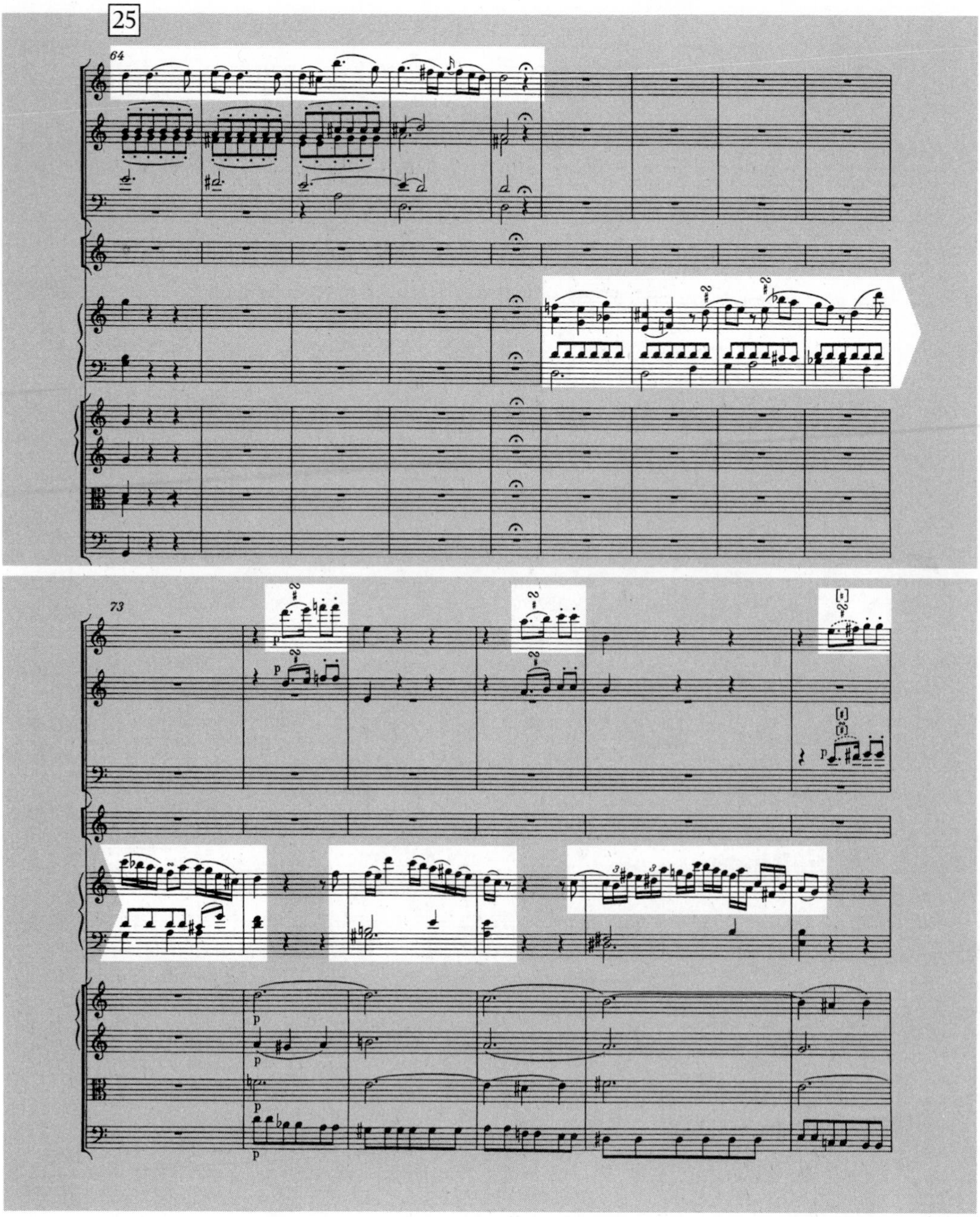
25
64
73
p

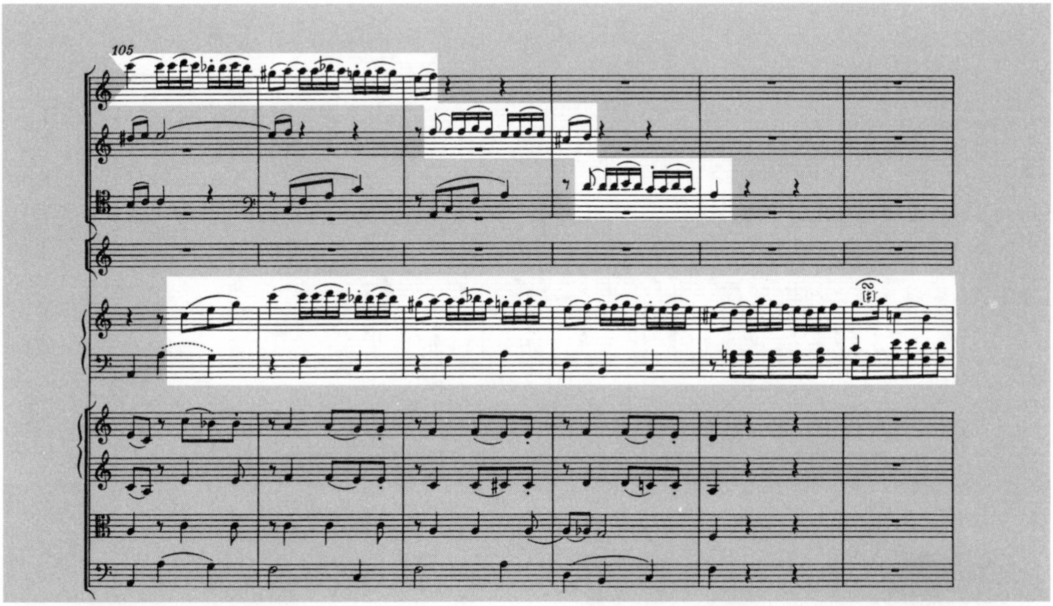
105

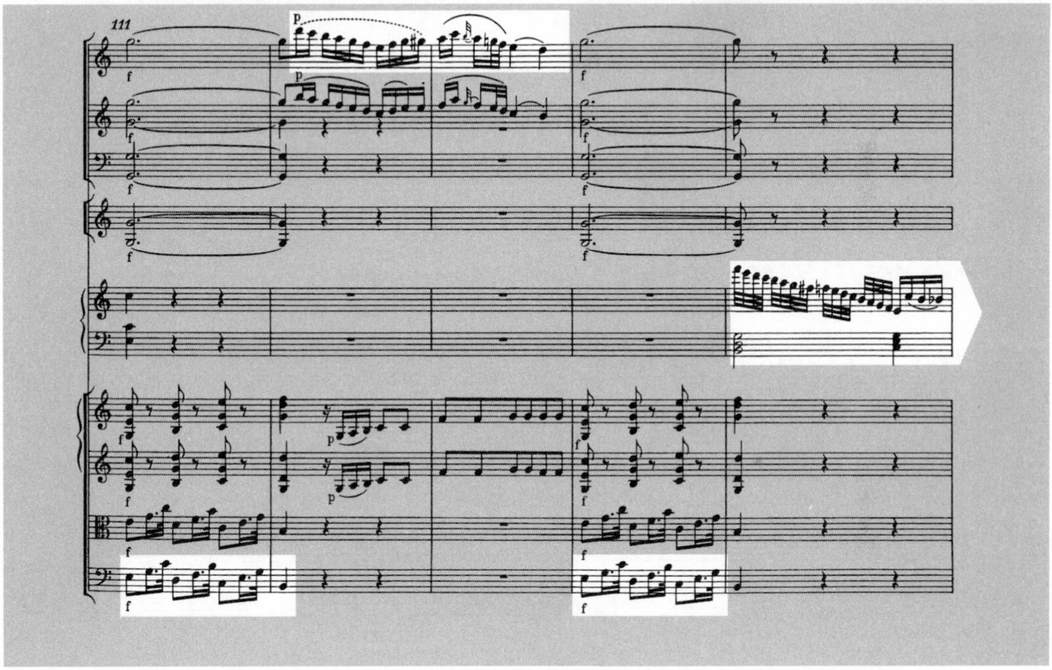
111

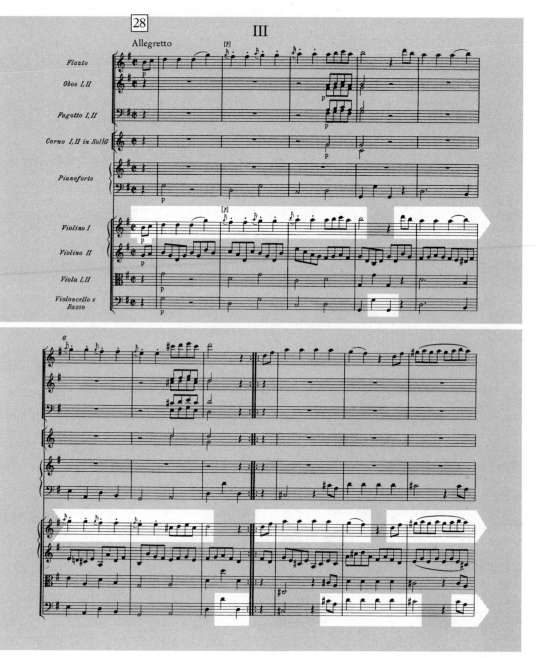

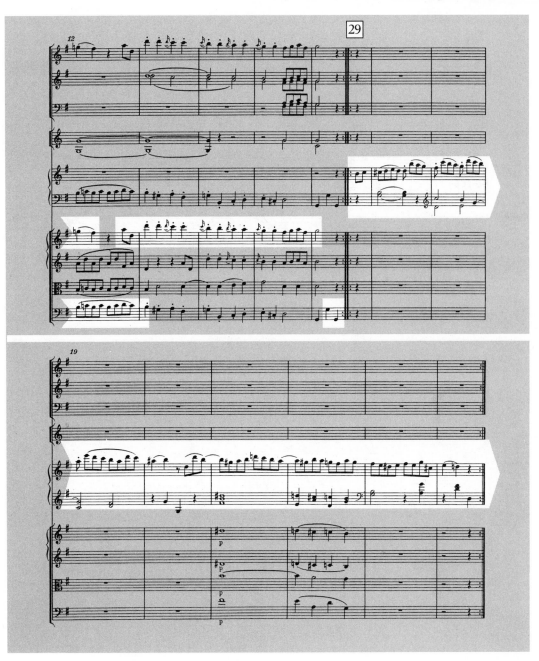

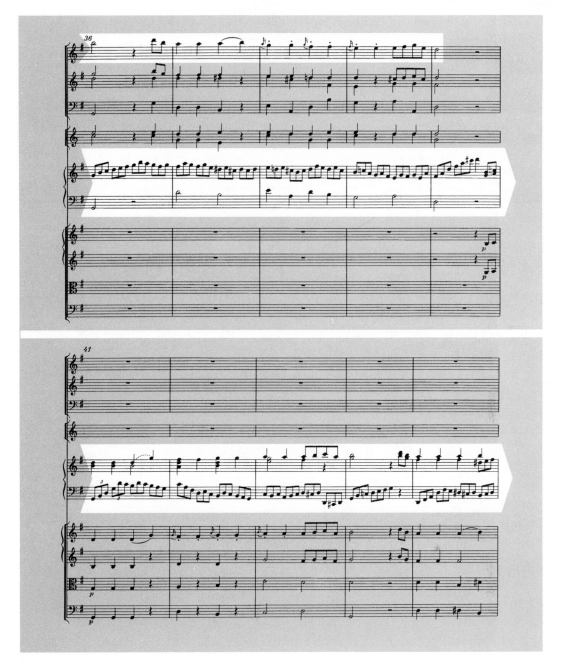

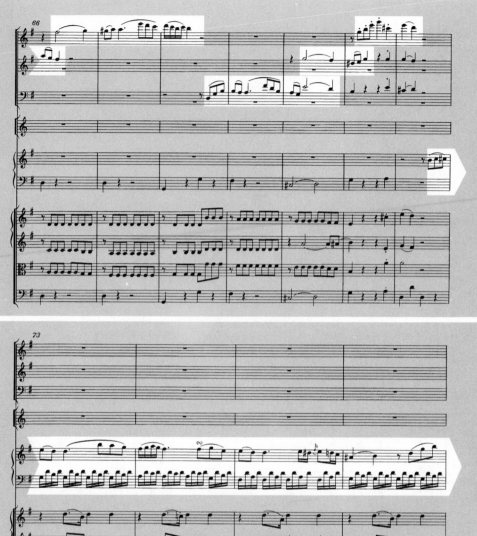

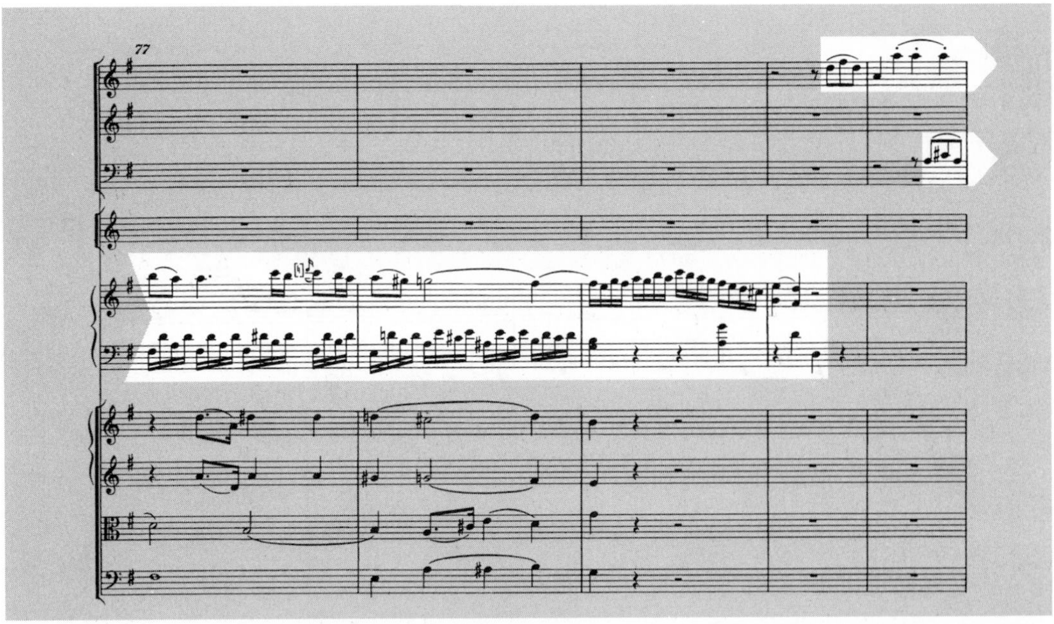
77

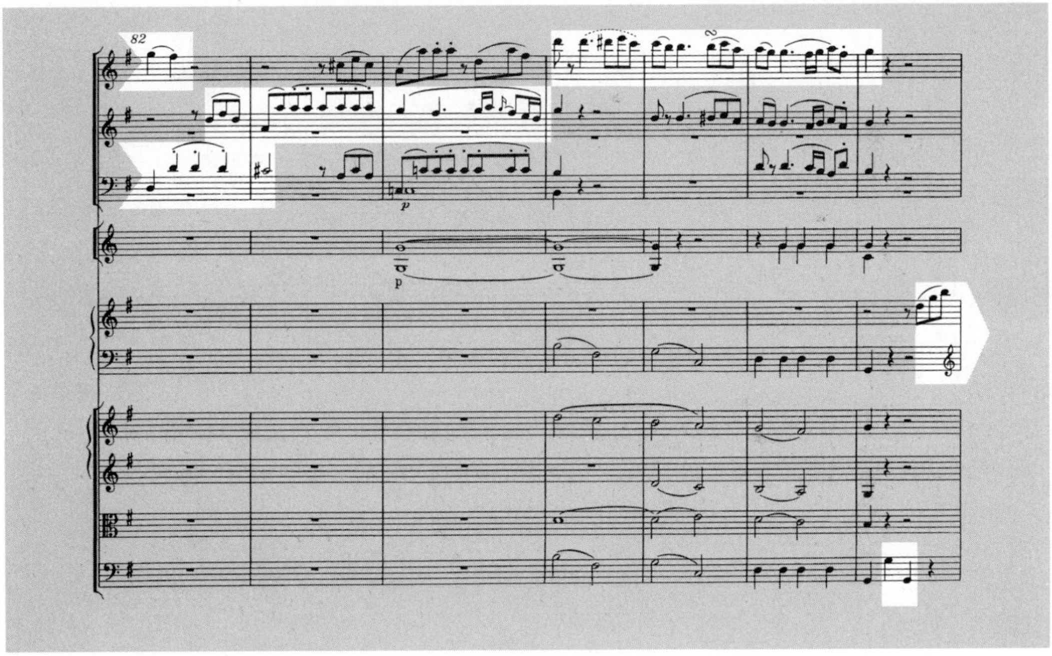
82
p
p

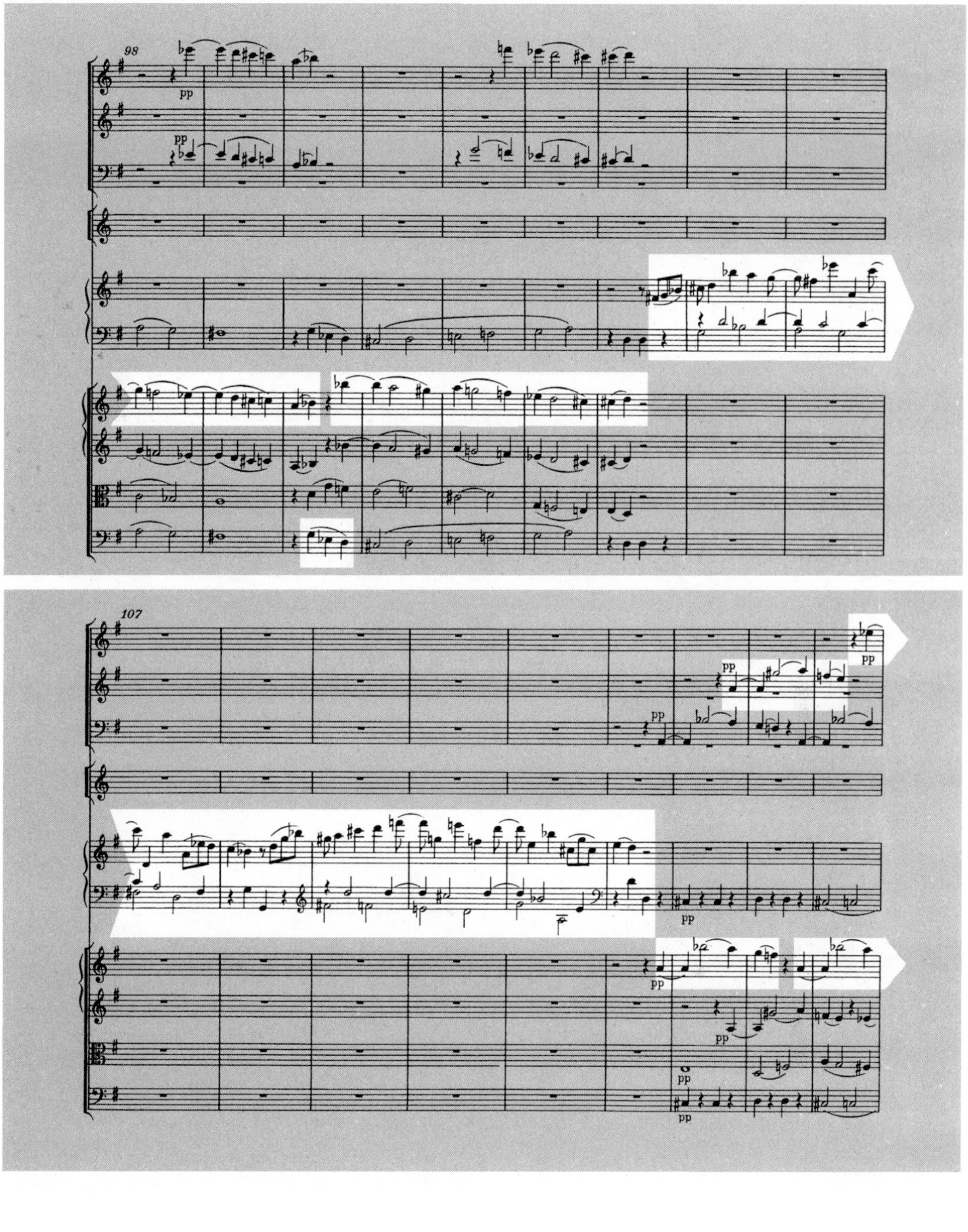
98
pp
pp
107
pp
pp
pp
pp
pp
pp
pp
pp

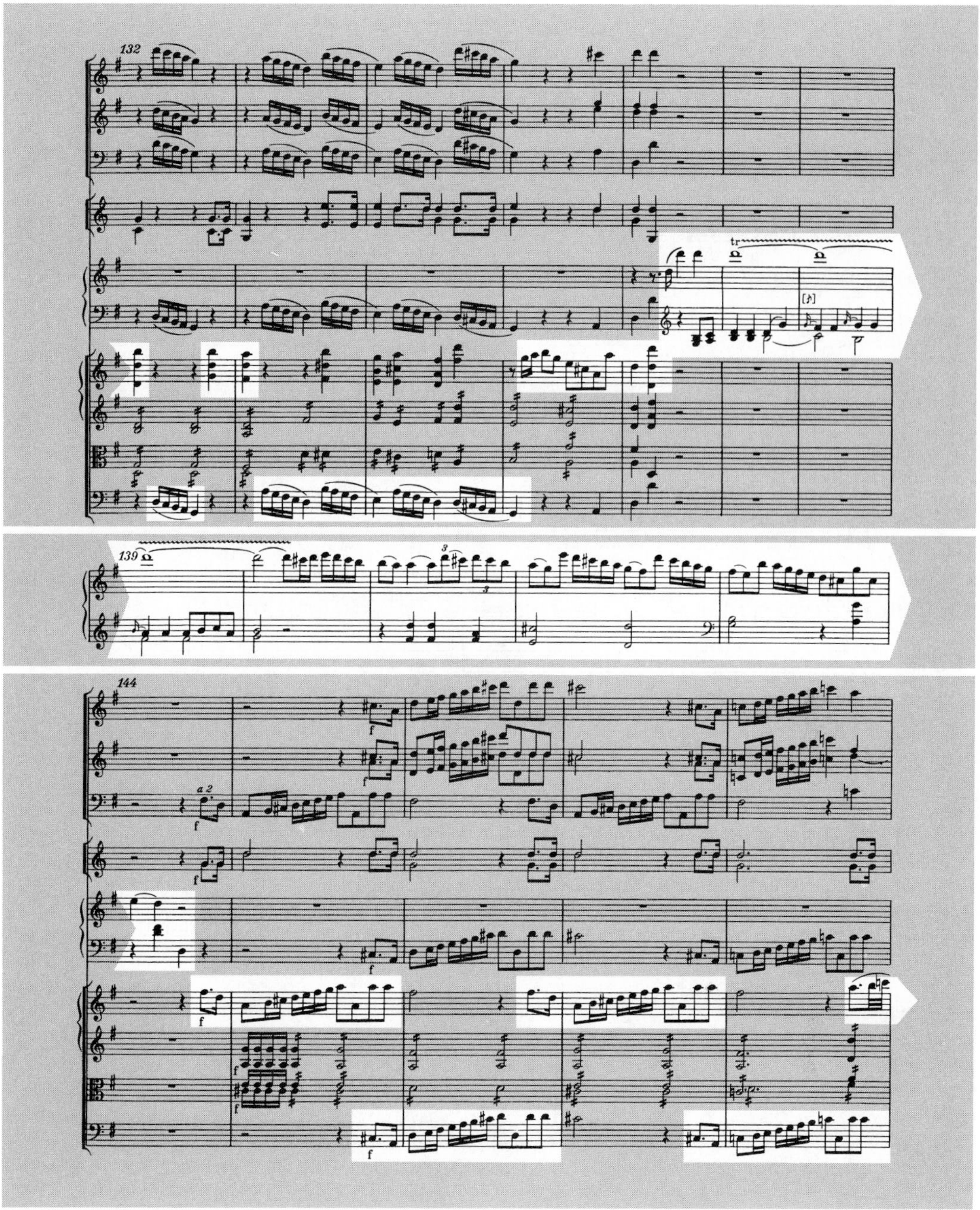
132
tr
139
144
a 2
f

32. Mozart, Piano Concerto in G major, K. 453: III

315
f
p
f
f
cre -
scendo
p
cre-
f
p
cre -
scendo
p
cre-
cre -
scendo
f
p
p
cre -
p
p
p
p

322
f
f
scendo
f
f
scendo
f
scendo
f
p
cresc.
f
p
cresc.
f
p
cresc.
f
p
cresc.
f
p
cresc.
f

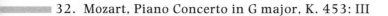

Mozart plays a critical role in the history of the piano concerto. Generally written for his own performance, Mozart's concertos mix the elegance of his own natural style with the virtuosic display and dramatic flair of Classical-era concert music. His most important formal contribution in the genre is the fusion of the Baroque ritornello procedures with the principles of Classical sonata-allegro form.

In the Piano Concerto in G major, K. 453, Baroque influences can be seen in its three-movement structure and in the alternation of *tutti* and solo sections. Within this Baroque framework, Mozart introduces elements of sonata-allegro form, including contrasting expositions by the *tutti* orchestra and solo piano, a development, and a recapitulation. The movement closes with a final *tutti* section that contains a cadenza composed by Mozart.

The form of the slow movement is similar to that of the first movement. The *tutti* begins with a haunting five-measure theme followed by a number of other thematic ideas. The pianist repeats the opening five-measure theme, but uses its harmonic ambiguity to begin moving to the dominant key. The first theme continues to mark important arrival points throughout the movement: it functions as a transition from the exposition to the development, it initiates the recapitulation, and, in an altered form, it signals the end of the movement.

The theme-and-variations final movement follows a typical scenario. The theme is a lighthearted rounded binary tune. The first two variations maintain the repeats of the original theme, while the final three variations have written-out repeats, alternating material between orchestra and soloist. The fourth variation is in the obligatory minor key, and the fifth provides a vigorous climax. The movement closes with an exuberant free fantasy that incorporates material from the principal theme.

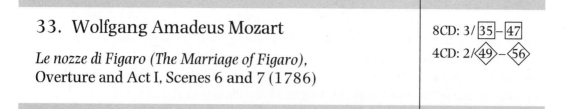

33. Wolfgang Amadeus Mozart

Le nozze di Figaro (The Marriage of Figaro),
Overture and Act I, Scenes 6 and 7 (1786)

8CD: 3/ 35 – 47
4CD: 2/ 49 – 56

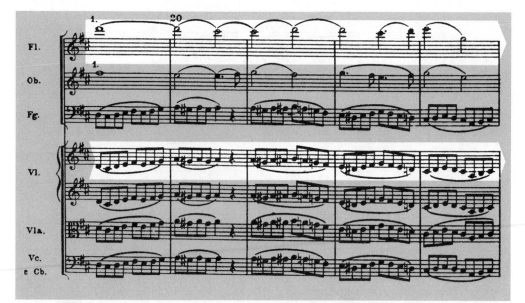

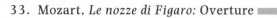

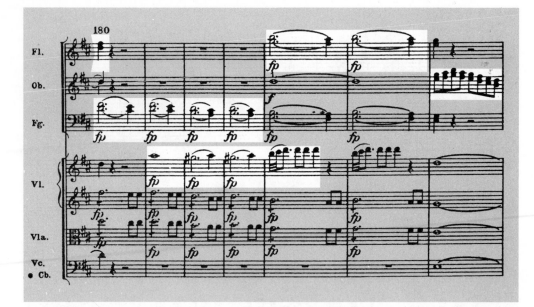

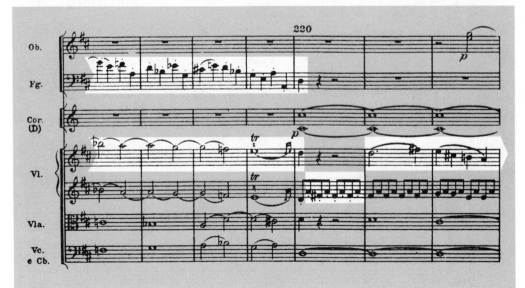

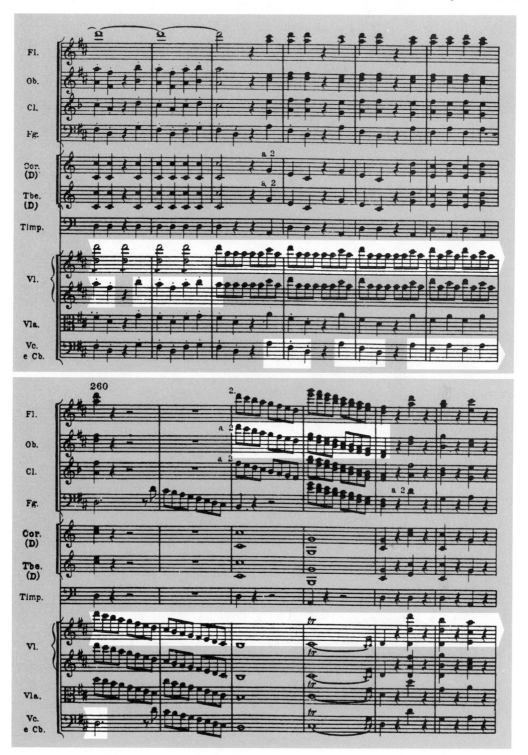

No. 6. "Non so più cosa son, cosa faccio"

por - ta - no via con se,___ por - ta - no via con
my ev - 'ry word and tone,___ my ev - 'ry word and

se,___ E se non ho chi m'o - da, e
tone.___ And if no one will lis - ten... and

se non ho chi m'o - da, par - lo d'a - mor con
if no one will lis - ten, then I will talk a -

me,___ con me,___ par - lo d'a - mor con me.
lone___ of love,___ talk to my - self a - lone.

Recitative

(as above)

li - ce! Tu ben sai quan-to io t'a - mo; a te Ba-si - lio tut-to già
hap - py! You must know how much I love you; I'm sure Ba-si - lio told you al -

dis - se. Or sen - ti, se per po - chi mo-men - ti me-co in giar-
read - y! Now lis - ten, if you on - ly con-sent to meet me to -

Basilio *(offstage)*

din sull' im-bru-nir del gior - no, ah per ques-to fa-vo-re io pa-ghe-rei. E u -
night in the gar-den of the cas - tle, I will am-ply re-pay you for this fa-vor. He

Count **Susanna** **Count**

sci - to po - co fa. Chi par - la? O De - i! E - sci,
left not long a - go. Ba - si - lio! Good Heav - ens! Hur - ry,

Susanna *(very agitated)* **Basilio** *(still offstage)*

ed al-cun non en - tri. Ch'io vi la - sci qui so - lo? Da ma-da - ma sa-rà,
don't let him en - ter. I should leave you a - lone here? He can't be ver-y far, per-

33. Mozart, *Le nozze di Figaro:* Recitative, "Ah, son perduto!"

Count *(pointing to the chair)*   **Susanna**

va - do a cer - car - lo.   Quì die - tro mi por - rò.   Non vi ce -
haps with the Count - ess.   I'll step be - hind this chair.   No, that's too

Count   **Susanna**   *(The Count*

la - te. Ta - ci, e cer - ca ch'ei par - ta.   Ohi - mè! che fa - te!
risk - y. Qui - et, get rid of him quick - ly.   Oh, Lord, how aw - ful!

tries to hide behind the arm-chair; Susanna stands between him and Cherubino; the Count draws her

Basilio *(Enters.)*

Su - san - na, il ciel vi sal - vi!   A - vre - ste a ca - so ve - du - to il
Su - san - na, Heav - en bless you!   Do you by chance know where the

gently away; meanwhile the page passes in front of the chair and crouches in it; Susanna covers

Susanna   **Basilio**

Con - te? E co - sa de - ve far me - co il   Con - te? A - ni - mo, u - sci - te.   A - spet -
Count is? And what on earth should the Count do   here?   Go now, I'm bus - y.   Just a

him with the dressing-gown.)

                                             Susanna

ta - te, sen - ti - te, Fi - ga - ro di lui cer - ca. (Oh cie - lo!)
min - ute, it seems that Fi - ga - ro wants to see him. The Count,

410

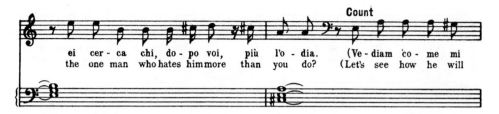

ei cer - ca chi, do - po voi, più l'o - dia. (Ve - diam co - me mi
the one man who hates him more than you do? (Let's see how he will

ser - ve.) Io non ho mai nel - la mo-ral sen - ti - to ch'u - no ch'a - ma la mo - glie o-
serve me.) That is not so. There is no such con - clu - sion, that if one loves the wife, one

di il ma - ri - to, per dir che il Con - te v'a - ma. Sor - ti - te, vil mi -
must hate the hus-band. In fact, my mas - ter loves you. Get out of here this

(resentfully)

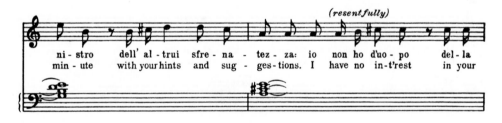

ni - stro dell' al - trui sfre - na - tez - za: io non ho d'uo - po del - la
min - ute with your hints and sug - ges - tions. I have no in - t'rest in your

Basilio

vo - stra mo - ra - le, del Con - te, del suo a - mor. Non c'è al - cun
lec - tures on mor - als, in your mas - ter, in his love. Don't take it

ma - le.   Ha cia-scun i suoi gu - sti.   Io mi cre - de - a che pre-fe-rir do -
that way.   I don't mean to of-fend you.   I was just think - ing that you   would pre-

ve-ste per a-man - te,   co-me fan tut-te quan - te,   un si-gnor li - be-ral, pru-den-te, e
fer the type of lov - er   which most wo-men ad - mire,   a   lord who is lib-er - al and

Susanna *(anxiously)* Basilio

sag - gio,   a un gio-vi-na - stro,   a un pag - gio. A Che-ru-bi - no? A Che-ru-
pru-dent,   to a young pip-squeak,   a   page-boy. Not Che-ru-bi - no? Yes, Che-ru-

bi - no,   Che-ru-bin d'a - mo - re,   ch'og - gi sul far del gior - no   pas-seg-
bi - no,   Che-ru-bin the Cu - pid,   who ear-li - er this morn - ing   was

Susanna *(forcefully)*

gia - va qui in - tor - no   per en - trar. Uom ma-li - gno, un' im-po-stu-ra è
prowl-ing near your door,   try-ing to   en - ter. You're a vil - lain, who tells ma - li - cious

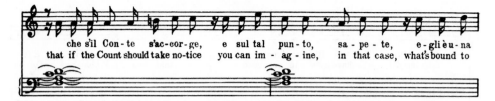

che s'il Con-te s'ac-cor-ge, e sul tal pun-to, sa-pe-te, e-gli è u-na
that if the Count should take no-tice you can im-ag-ine, in that case, what's bound to

Susanna

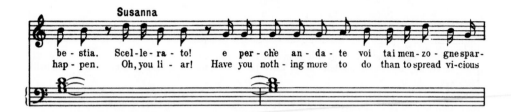

be-stia. Scel-le-ra-to! e per-chè an-da-te voi tai men-zo-gne spar-
hap-pen. Oh, you li-ar! Have you noth-ing more to do than to spread vi-cious

Basilio

gen-do? Io! che in-giu-sti-zia! Quel che com-pro io ven-do, a
gos-sip? I! You're mis-tak-en, I just sell what I pur-chase, I

quel che tut-ti di-co-no, io non ci ag-giun-go un pe-lo.
ech-o what they all say, not add-ing in the slight-est.

Count (*Steps forward.*)   **Basilio**   **Susanna**

Co-me! che di-con tut-ti? Oh bel-la! Oh cie-lo!
Real-ly! What are they say-ing? (De-light-ful!) Ah, Heav-ens!

No. 7. "Cosa sento! Tosto andate"

Count (to Basilio)

Co - sa sen - to!
That's the lim - it!

To - sto an - da - te,
Go this min - ute,

e scac-cia-te
find the cul-prit

il se - dut - tor,
and throw him out,

to - sto an -
go and

da - te, e scac-cia-te il se - dut-tor.
find him, and throw the cul - prit out.

Basilio

In mal pun-to
How ill - cho-sen

son qui giun - to; per - do - na - te, o mio si -
was my sto - ry, just a ru - mor, with - out a

Susanna

gnor. Che ru - i - na! me me - schi - na! son' op - pres - sa dal do -
doubt. We'll be ru - ined by the scan - dal if this gos - sip gets a -

lor!
bout!

Basilio

In mal pun - to
How ill - cho - sen

Count

To - sto an - da - te, an - da - te,
Don't de - lay an - y long - er,

Che ru - i - na!
This is aw - ful!

son qui giun - to, per - do - na - te, o
was my sto - ry, just a ru - mor, with -

e scac - cia - te il se - dut - tor.
go and throw the scoun - drel out.

(half fainting)

Me me - schi - na! me me - schi - na! Son' op -
What will hap - pen! Heav - en help us! I am

mio si - gnor.
out a doubt.

pres - sa dal do - lor, son' op - pres - sa dal do -
feel - ing ver - y faint, I am feel - ing ver - y

33. Mozart, *Le nozze di Figaro:* Terzetto, "Cosa sento!"

giu - sti Dei, che mai sa - rà!
no one knows how_ this will end.

(to the Count, with malice)

non c'è al - cu - na_ ño - vi - tà. Ah, del pag - gio
they will nev - er_ show their hand. What I told you

or ca - pi - sco_ co - me va!
now I see_ how_ mat - ters stand.

quel che ho det - to, e - ra so - lo un mio so -
was a ru - mor, mere sus - pi - cion with no foun -

Ac - ca-der non può di peg-gio, ah, no, ah, no! giu-sti
Noth - ing worse than this could hap-pen, ah, no, ah, no! No one

spet-to.
da-tion.

Co - sì fan tut-te le bel-le,
That's the way all wo-men do it,

O - ne - stis - si - ma si - gno - ra,
Now at last __ my eyes __ are o - pen,

cresc.

f

Dei, che mai sa-rà, che mai sa-rà! Ac - ca -
knows how this will end, how this will end! Noth - ing

non c'e al-cu-na no-vi-tà, co - sì
they will nev-er show their hand. That's the

or ca - pi - sco co - me va! o - ne -
now I see __ how mat - ters stand. Now at

p

der non può di peg-gio, giu - sti Dei,_ che_
worse than this could hap-pen, no one knows how_

fan tut - te le bel - le, non c'è al - cu - na
way all wo - men do it, they will nev - er_

stis - si - ma si - gno-ra, or ca - pi - sco_
last_ my eyes are o - pen, now I see_ how_

mai sa - rà, giu - sti Dei,_ che_ mai sa - rà, giu - sti
this will end, no one knows how_ this will end, this af -

no - vi - tà, non c'è al - cu - na_ no - vi - tà, non c'è al -
show their hand, they will nev - er_ show their hand, they will

co - me va, or ca - pi - sco_ co - me va, or ca -
mat - ters stand, now I see_ how_ mat - ters stand, now I

che mai sa - rà, che ____ sa - rà, che ____ sa -
is out of hand, out ____ of hand, out ____ of

cu - na no - vi - tà, no - vi - tà, no - vi -
nev - er show their hand, show ____ their hand, show ____ their

pi - sco co - me va, co - me va, co - me
see how mat - ters stand, mat - ters stand, mat - ters

p calando

rà, che ___ sa - rà!
hand, out ____ of hand.

tà, no - vi - tà!
hand, show ____ their hand.

va, co - me va!
stand, mat - ters stand.

pp

Le nozze di Figaro (The Marriage of Figaro) (1786) is a brilliant comic opera (*opera buffa*) based on a libretto by Lorenzo da Ponte. Adapted from a controversial Beaumarchais play, the opera sparkles with wit and satire. While the story is basically a bedroom farce, Mozart creates a theatrical masterpiece with his depth of characterization, sublime music, and innovative ensemble treatment.

The overture, which establishes the quick pace and jovial mood of the opera, is set in a modified sonata-allegro form. The exposition and recapitulation are tuneful and clearly delineated, but the development section is omitted. Additional modifications can be seen in the absence of repeats in the exposition and the lack of closure at the end, when the overture segues into the first scene.

The music for Act I, Scene 6, begins with Cherubino's ardent aria "Non so più." Cherubino is a young boy who has discovered women. In love with the Countess, he sings a song about love to her servant Susanna. In keeping with his youthful character, the song maintains simplicity of form **(A-B-A-C)** and texture. The pulsating string accompaniment suggests the excited, breathless state of Cherubino. Some of the humor in this scene stems from Mozart's assignment of a mezzo-soprano to the character of Cherubino, one of the most amusing and enjoyable examples of a "trouser role" in all of opera.

In the delightful *secco* recitative that follows, the Count comes to woo Susanna. Cherubino, not wanting to be seen, takes refuge behind a large chair. The entrance of Basilio, the voice teacher, prompts the Count to hide behind the same chair, while Cherubino stealthily climbs into the chair under a dress. Basilio's idle chatter eventually angers the Count, and he comes out of hiding—to the delight of the music master.

Act I, Scene 7, is a trio, one of several celebrated ensembles in the opera. In these musical numbers, Mozart is able to create operatic scenes in which the drama is advanced without sacrificing the music. The trio for Susanna, the Count, and Basilio can be seen as an extended sonata-allegro form. After the initial statements in B-flat major, Susanna attempts to distract the men from Cherubino's presence by pretending to faint. Mozart supports her diversion with a modulation to the dominant as the men admire her figure. But Susanna's efforts are in vain, and the Count uncovers Cherubino while relating an earlier episode about the young man. The opening material returns, and now Susanna is unable to detour the Count and Basilio from the tonic key.

34. Wolfgang Amadeus Mozart

Eine kleine Nachtmusik (A Little Night Music),
K. 525 (1787)

8CD: 3/ 48 – 67
4CD: 1/ 60 – 79

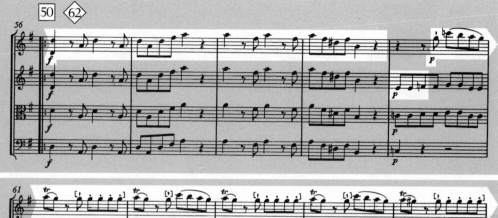

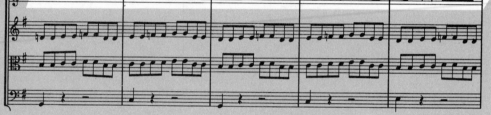

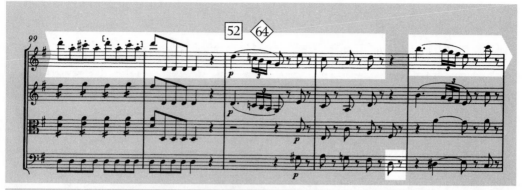

II. Romance

Andante

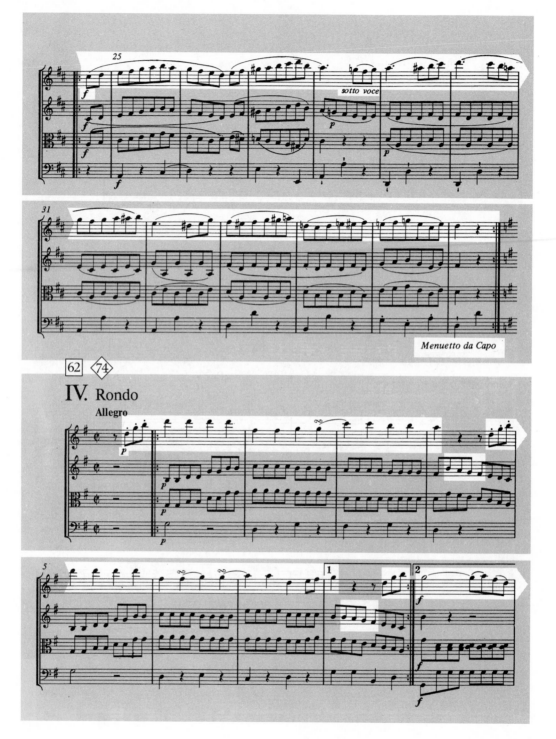

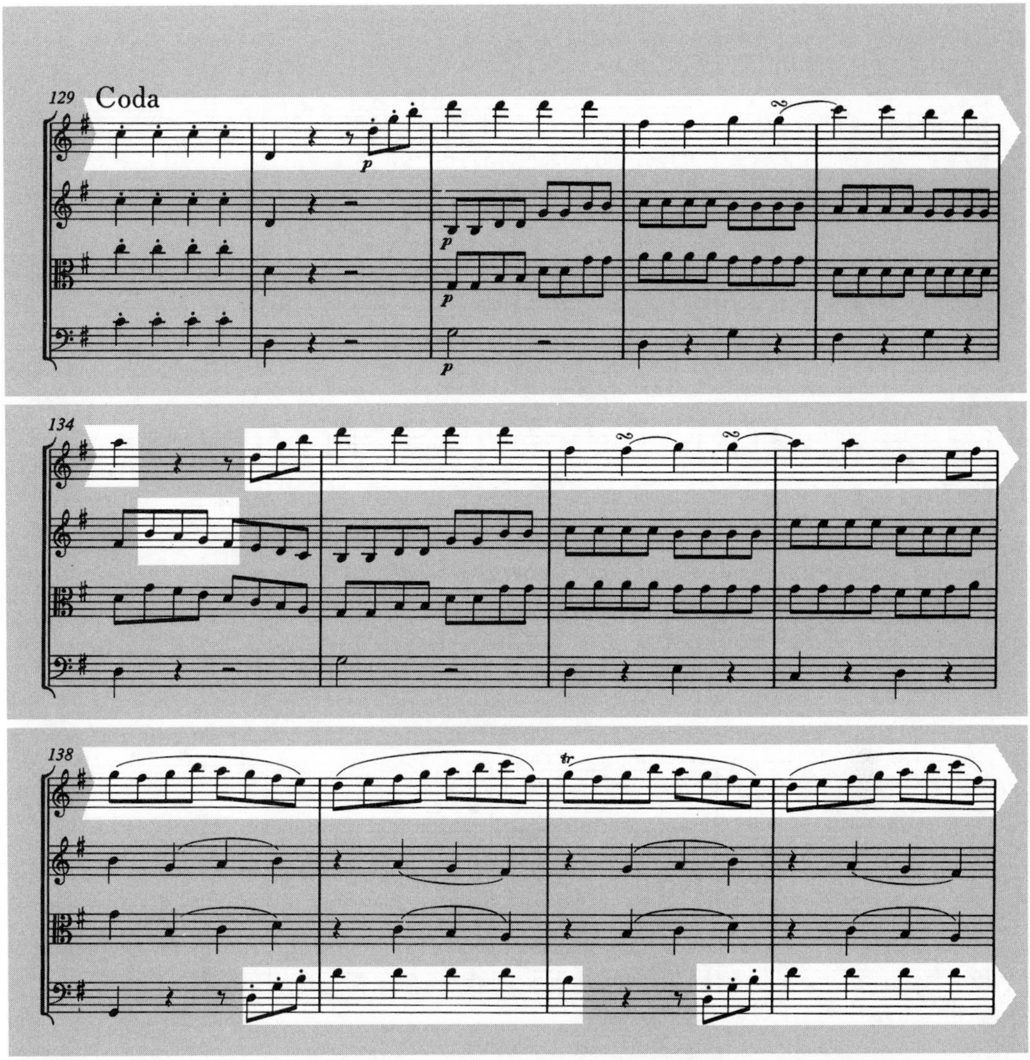
129
Coda
p
p
p
p
134
138
tr
142
tr

The instrumental serenade is a light entertainment work related to the divertimento. The term "serenade" suggests a nighttime performance, which is also reflected in the subtitle of Mozart's Serenade in D major, *Eine kleine Nachtmusik (A Little Night Music)*, although this title probably does not originate from Mozart. Like the divertimento, the serenade has no standard number of movements. *Eine kleine Nachtmusik* was originally created with five movements, but Mozart dropped one of the two minuets. As a result, the four remaining movements parallel the standard format of a symphony. While the nature of this work allows for a performance by a chamber ensemble, a chamber orchestral performance is Mozart's likely intention.

Although seemingly a simple work, *Eine kleine Nachtmusik* defines an important facet of Mozart's style with its tunefulness, elegance, and economical construction. The sonata-allegro first movement abounds with melodic motives. Three separate ideas are presented in the first theme alone, and both the second theme and closing theme provide strong contrasts. In a masterful stroke, all of the material of the exposition returns in the recapitulation essentially unaltered except for the subtle change in measure 99 that allows the remaining material to stay in the tonic. The development, which primarily focuses on the closing theme, and the coda are relatively brief and provide some harmonic contrast with chromatic inflections. In keeping with the tradition of binary structure, Mozart marks a repeat for the second half, which is sometimes observed in modern-day performances.

The middle movements are both set in clearly delineated forms. Typical of the instrumental Romanza, the second movement has a slow tempo, a lyrical principal theme, and a rondo structure. The minuet follows the standard structure. Most striking are the contrasts of moods between the vigorous opening, the elegant trio melody, and the subtle chromaticism near the end of the trio.

The delightful last movement deviates from standard classical forms. Labeled as a Rondo by Mozart, the Allegro can be seen as a hybrid structure with characteristics of both sonata-rondo and sonata-allegro forms. Regardless of the formal ambiguities, the lighthearted nature, flashy string technique, and subtle references to motives from earlier movements make this a brilliant finale to the work as a whole.

35. Wolfgang Amadeus Mozart

Symphony No. 40 in G minor, K. 550,
First Movement (1788)

8CD: 4/ 1 – 5

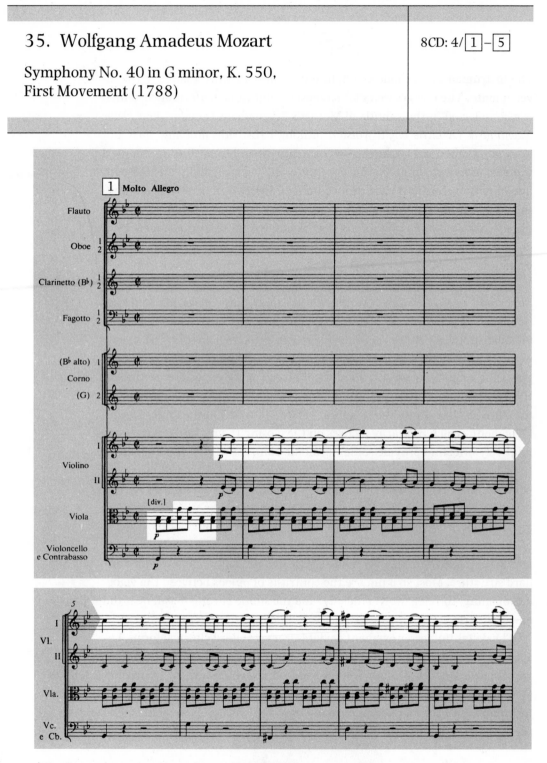

Editor's note: Square brackets indicate editorial additions.

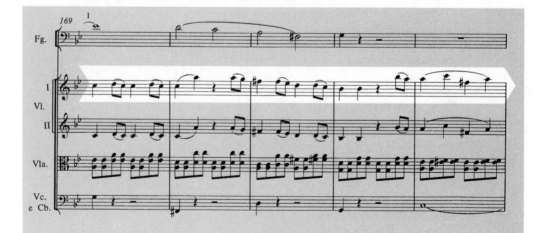

One of the most important developments of the Classical era was the emergence of the symphony. While three-movement works were not unusual in the genre at this time, the Viennese Classical style established a four-movement structure as the norm: sonata-allegro, slow movement, minuet, and fast finale. This format can be found in Mozart's last three symphonies (1788), which includes his darkest and most passionate work in the genre—the Symphony No. 40 in G minor.

Opening with a simple harmonic accompaniment, the first movement, in sonata-allegro form, presents a stark opening theme built around a simple three-note motive. Both the rhythm of this motive and its reiterated half-step are important thematic ideas that are developed throughout the movement. The contrasting second theme appears in B-flat major, the relative major, during the exposition, but Mozart brings it back in G minor during the recapitulation, where its chromatic descents create a poignant mood. Unlike most minor-mode symphonies of the Classical era, Mozart maintains the minor key through its vigorous final cadence.

36. Ludwig van Beethoven

Piano Sonata in C minor, Op. 13 *(Pathétique)*
(1798)

8CD: 4/ 6 – 23
4CD:2/ 44 – 48

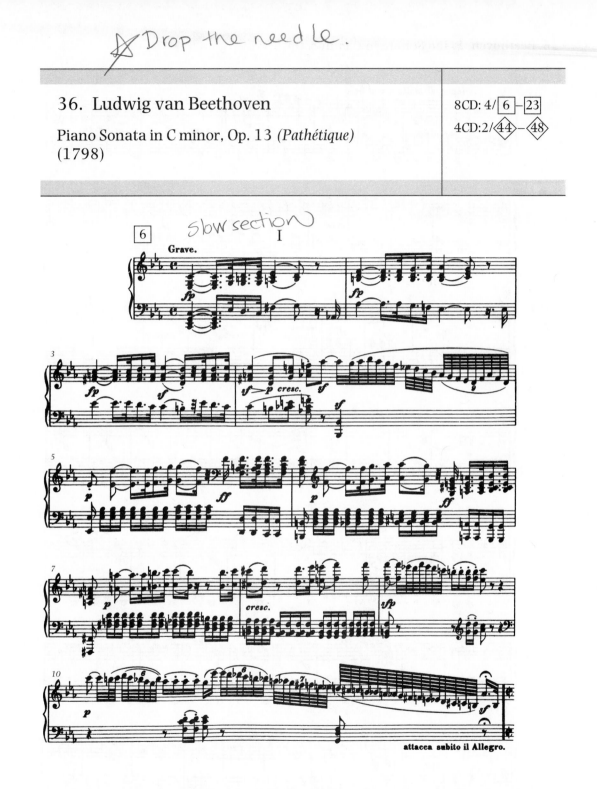

coda

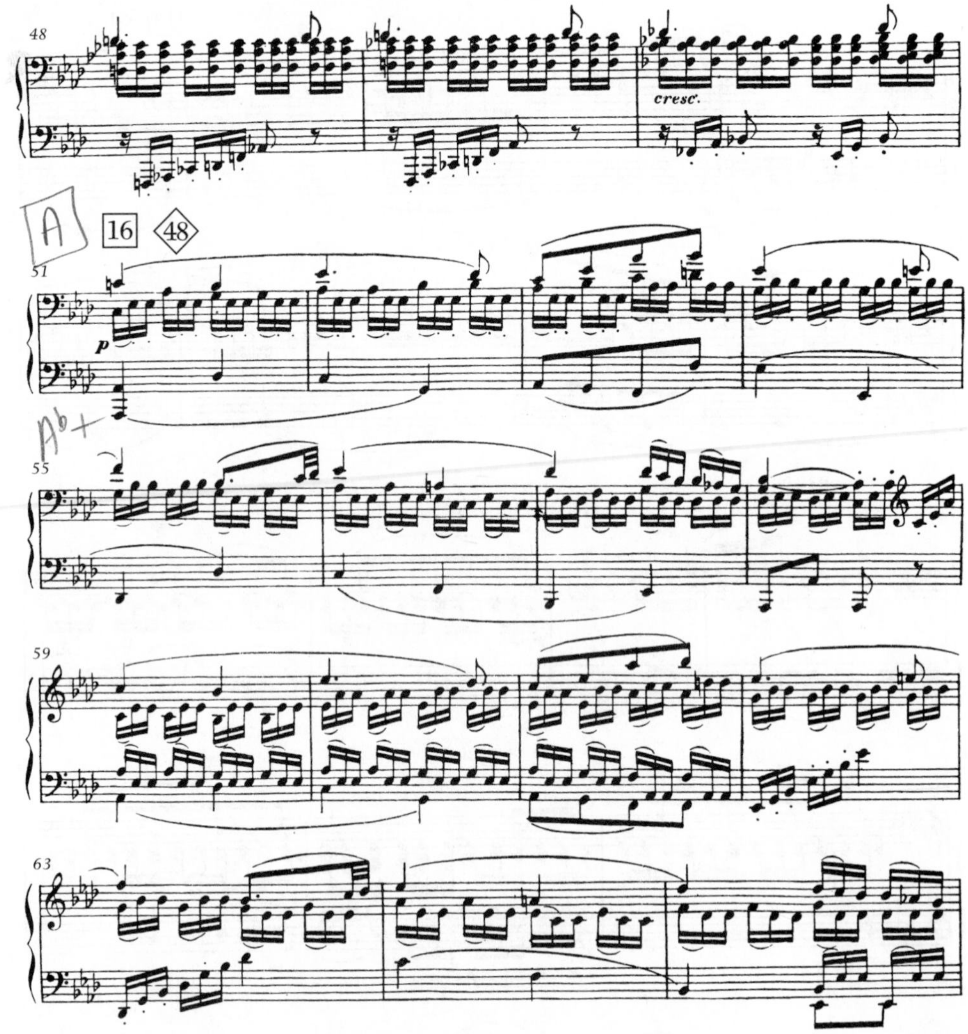
48
cresc.
16
48
51
p
55
59
63
66
pp
69
rf
rf
rf
pp

subject from 1st mvt.

III

C development?
new theme (like one

20

connector

coda

The *Pathétique* Sonata exhibits a wide range of emotional qualities. Using powerful symphonic gestures, intimate lyricism, and theatrical virtuosity, Beethoven (1770–1827) creates a variety of moods within an overall dark, brooding character. Symphonic qualities are most evident in the first movement, with the volatile, slow introduction, major-minor juxtapositions, and tremolo-like accompaniment. Two unusual features of the sonata-allegro structure are the initial arrival of the minor dominant key and the reappearance of the slow introduction at the beginning of the development and prior to the coda. A fragment of the introduction theme is treated in the development as well.

The sublime, lyrical second movement is set as a rondo: **A-B-A-C-A**. The recurring opening theme creates a strong sense of serenity. A second, contrasting section, beginning in A-flat minor, is more agitated, and its triplet rhythmic motion is retained in the final statement of **A**.

The finale returns to the dramatic, virtuosic mood of the first movement. The rondo finale follows the typical 7-part pattern: **A-B-A-C-A-B-A**. The energetic flow of constant eighth notes, triplets, and sixteenth notes pauses only briefly for the abbreviated second theme, and a more extended theme in section **C**. Contributing to the bleak quality of the movement is its unusual setting in the minor mode, which is sustained through the final cadence.

37. Ludwig van Beethoven

Violin Concerto in D major, Op. 61, Third Movement (1806)

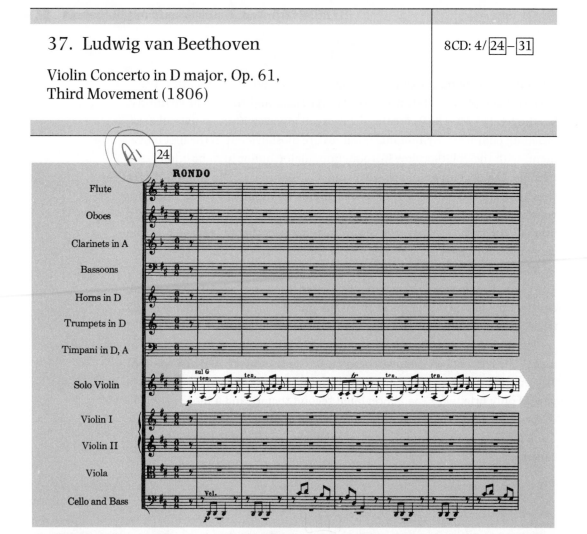

17
Fl.
TUTTI
ten.
tr
Ob.
ten.
Clar.
Fag.
Cor.
ten.
Trombe
Timp.
ff
p
p Vel.
unis.

26
ten.
a2
sf

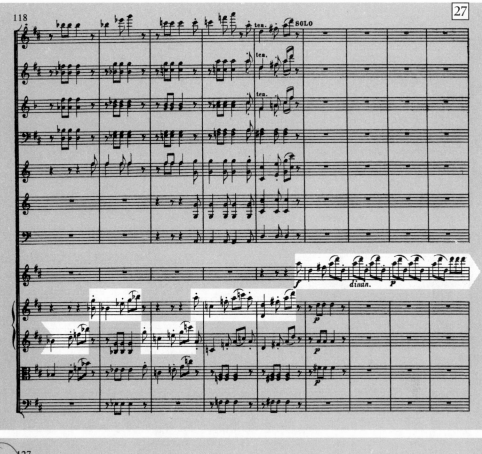

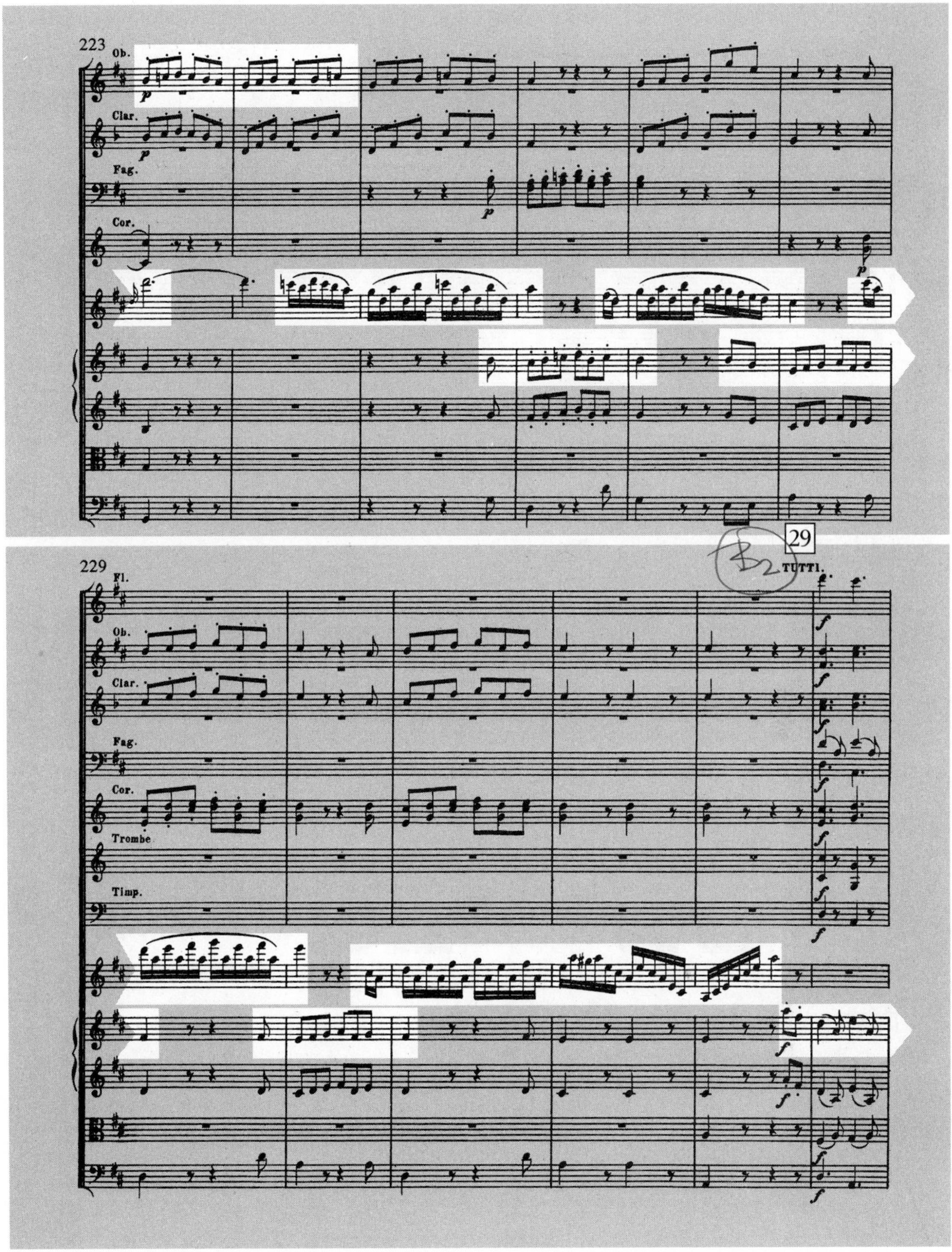
223
Ob.
Clar.
Fag.
Cor.
229
Fl.
Ob.
Clar.
Fag.
Cor.
Trombe
Timp.
29
TUTTI.

The delightful last movement of Beethoven's Violin Concerto in D major is set as a rondo: **A-B-A-C-A-B-A.** As in a sonata-allegro form, the initial **B** section modulates to the dominant, and the second statement remains in the tonic. Although section **C** has some of the harmonic character of a development section, it primarily centers on a new theme heard in two phrases alternating between the solo violin and bassoon.

Much of the humor and energy of this movement stem from the opening theme. Based on a five-note motive, the theme quickly moves through two statements of antecedent-consequent phrases. But each tonic arrival is immediately contradicted by a questioning open cadence, and the tonic is completely avoided in the third repetition, which initiates a modulation. The next two **A** sections are presented in the same manner, but following a dazzling, playful coda, the orchestra puts an end to the evasiveness with a forceful final cadence.

38. Ludwig van Beethoven

Symphony No. 5 in C minor, Op. 67
(1807–8)

—very balanced

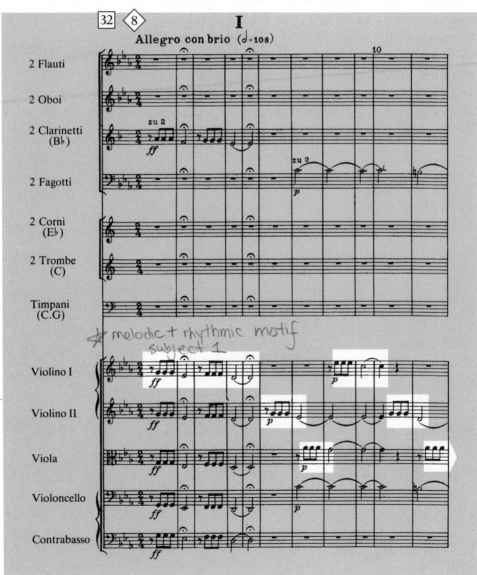

— question answer ideas.

☆ melodic + rhythmic motif subject 1

theme 2

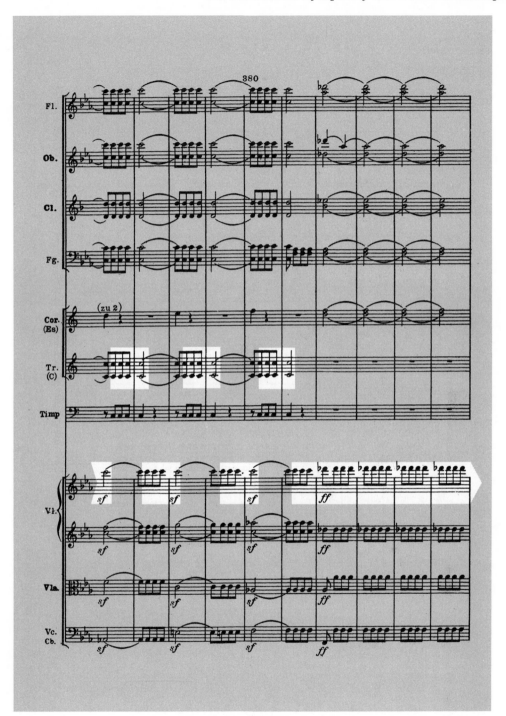

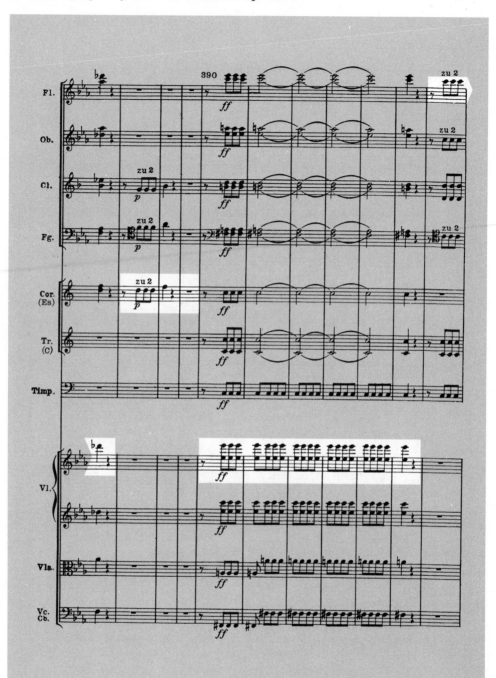

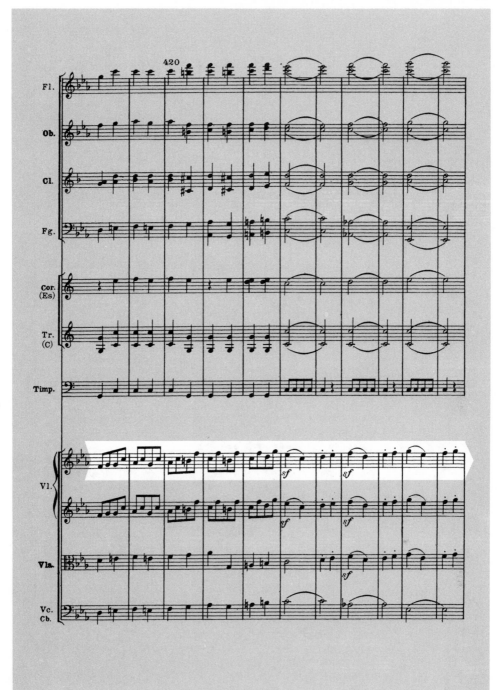

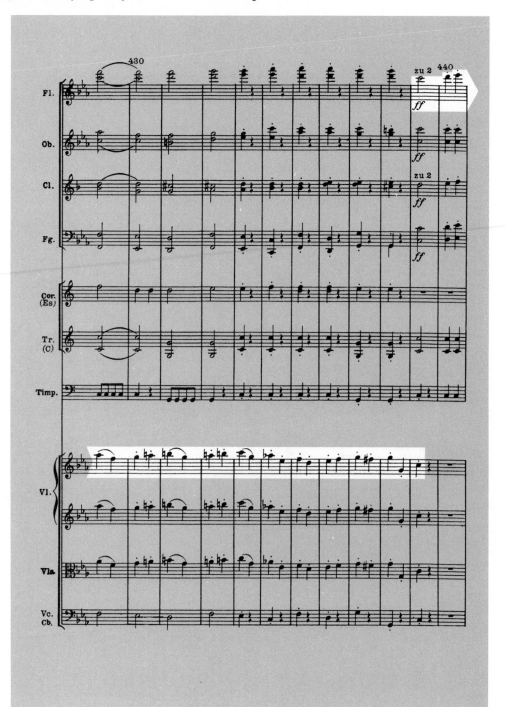

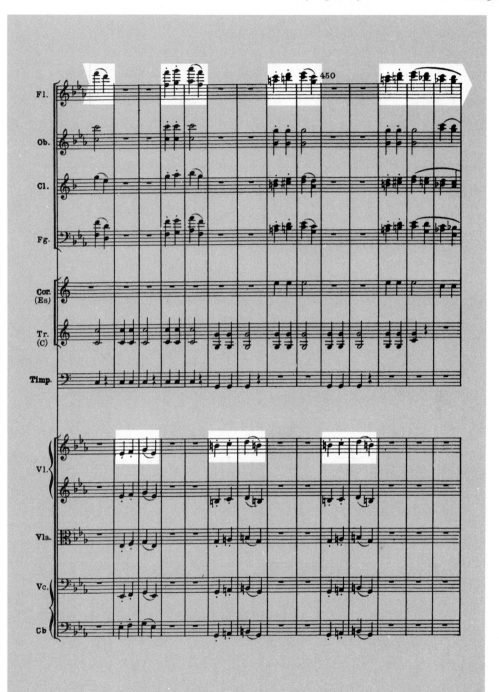

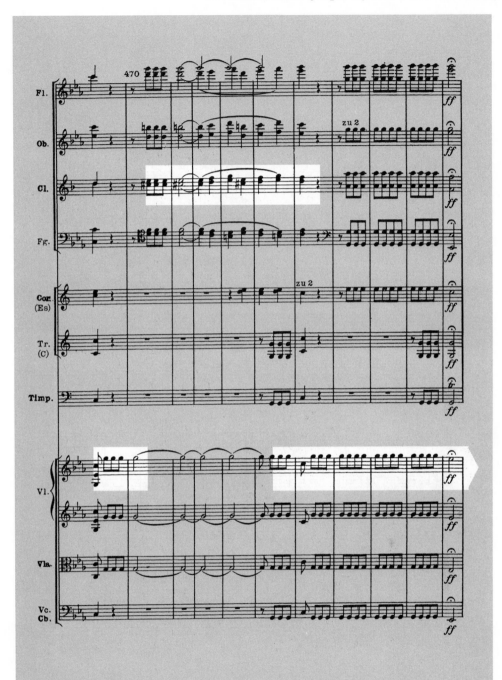

theme + variations. — *dotted rhythms*

II

38 14

Andante con moto (♪ = 92)

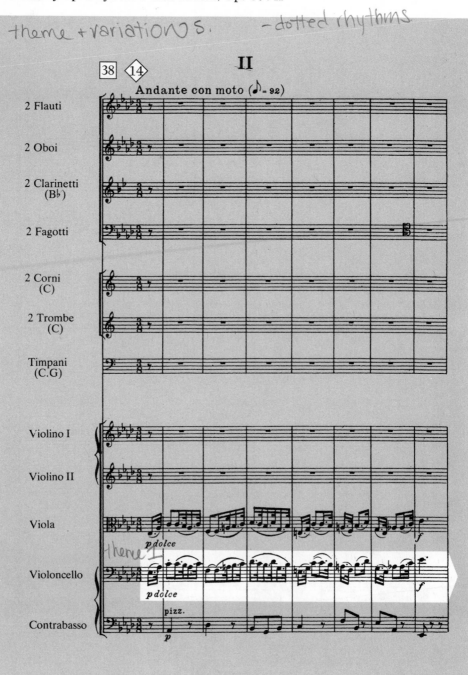

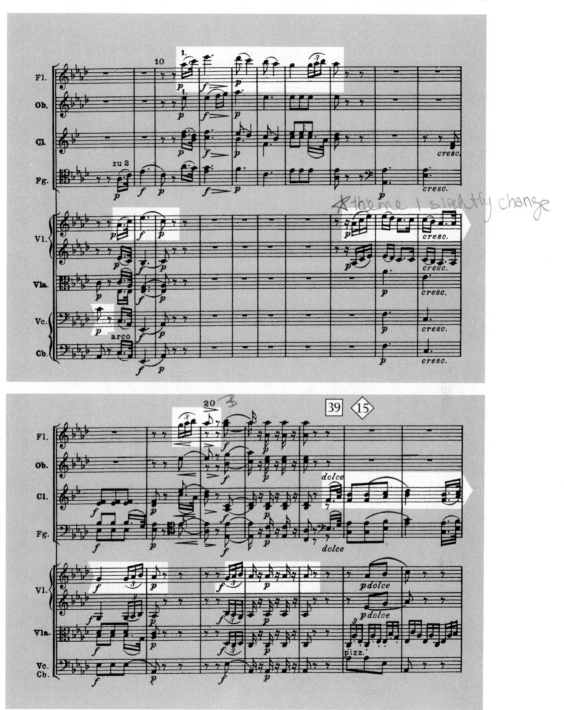

Variation 1

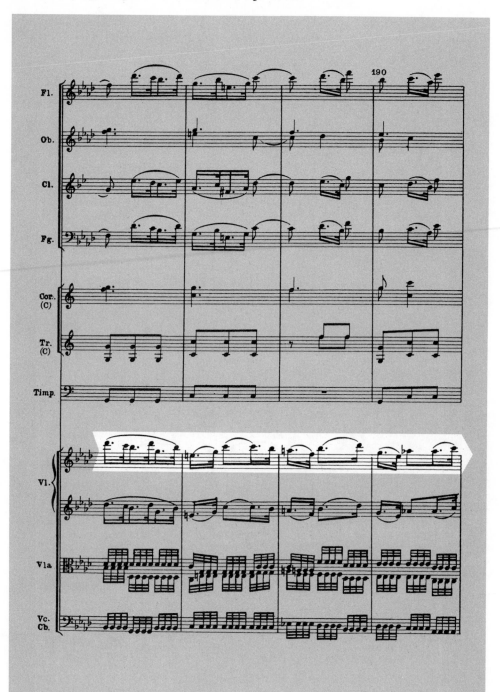

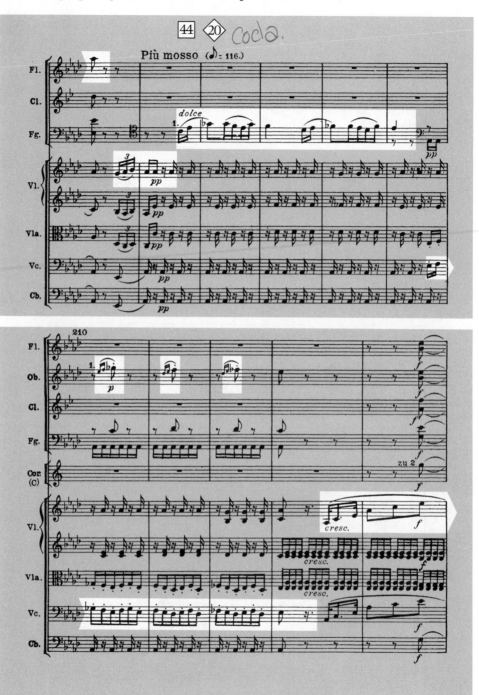

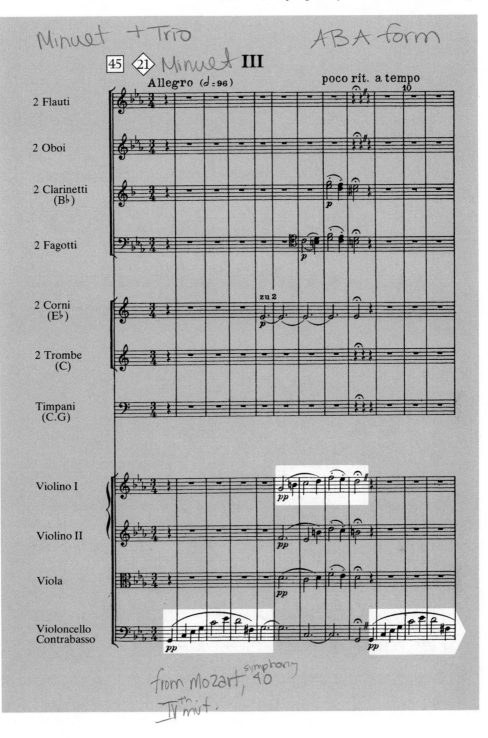

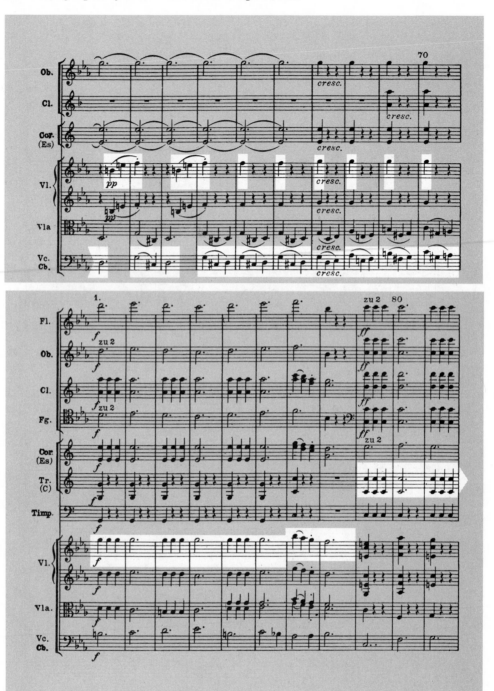

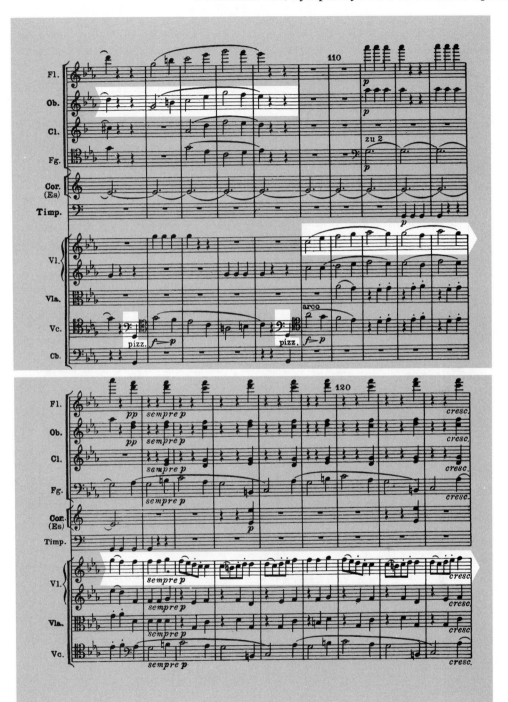

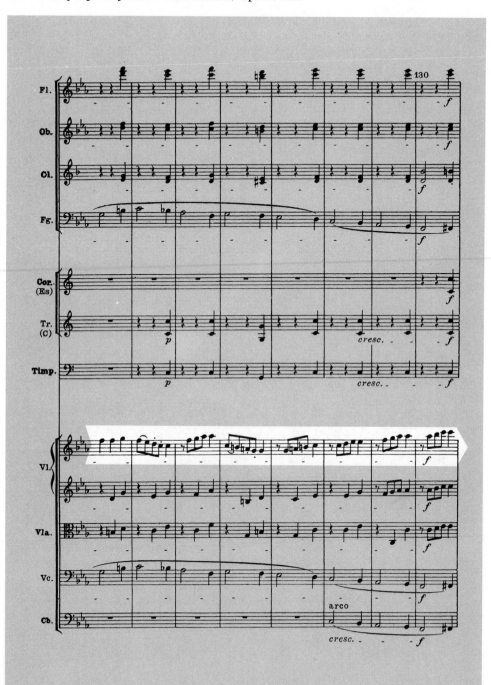

breaks fugue apart

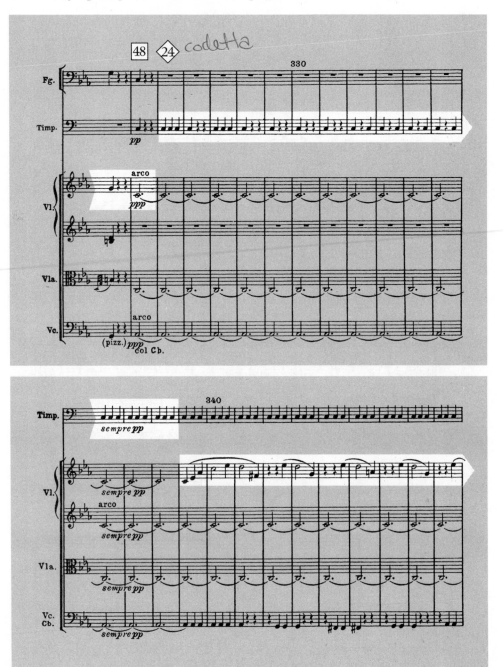

49
25
IV
Allegro (𝅗𝅥 = 84)
Piccolo
2 Flauti
2 Oboi
2 Clarinetti (C)
2 Fagotti
zu 2
Contrafagotto
2 Corni (C)
2 Trombe (C)
Alto
Tenore
3 Tromboni
Basso
Timpani (C.G)
Violino I
Violino II
Viola
Violoncello
Contrabasso
ff

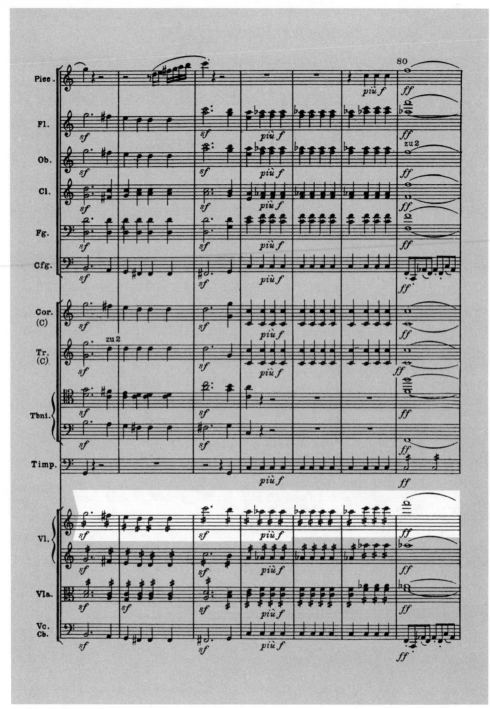

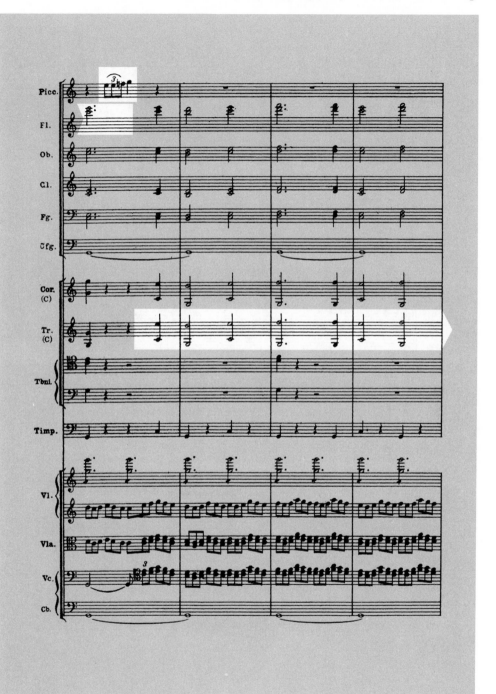

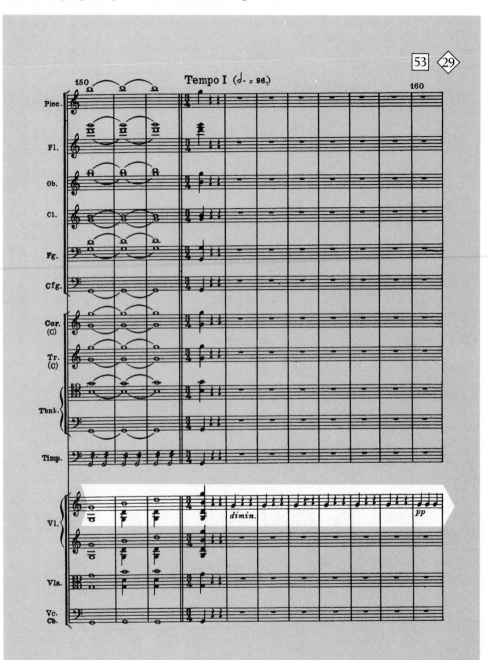

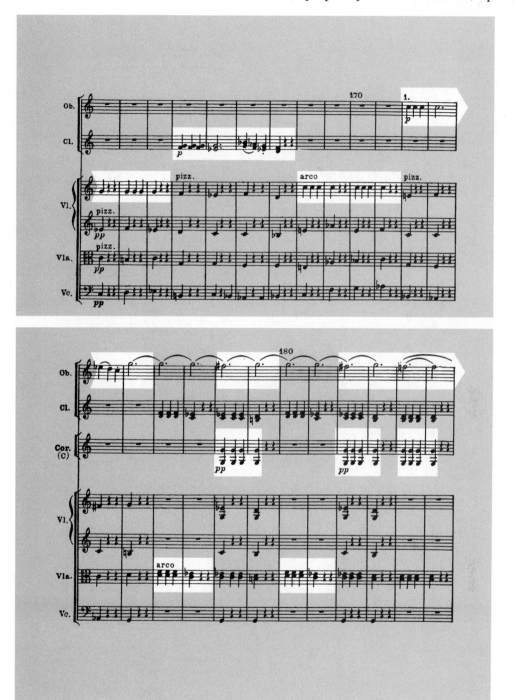

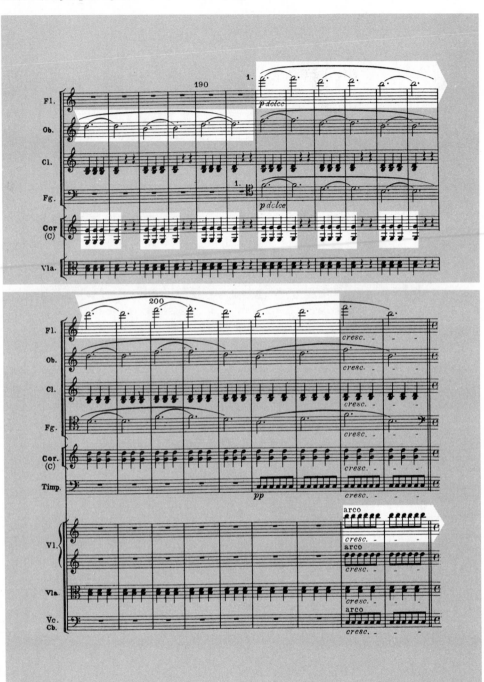

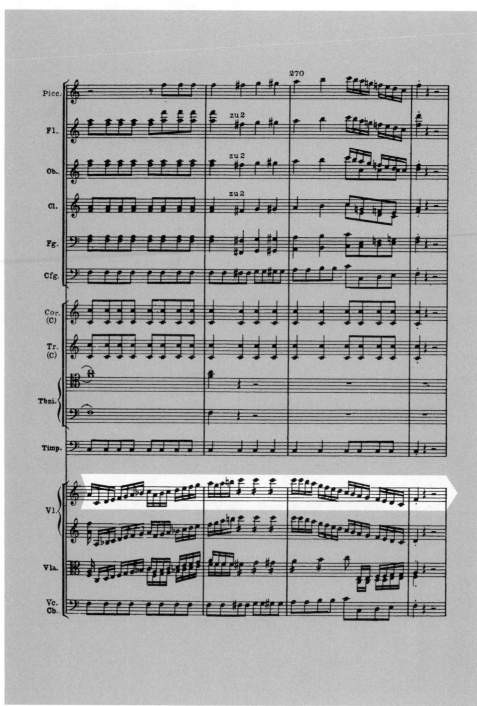

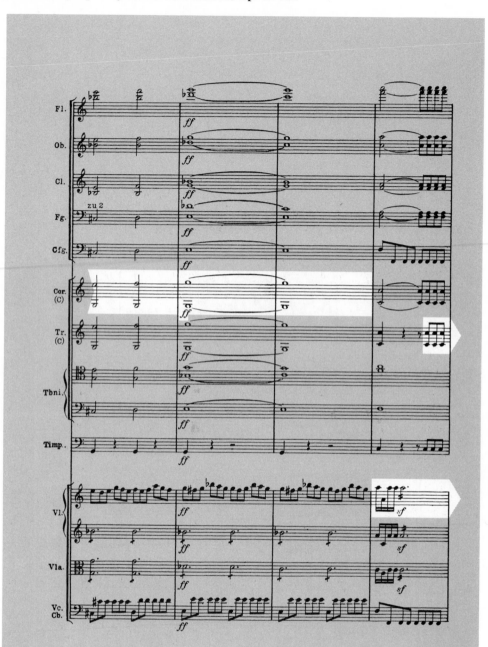

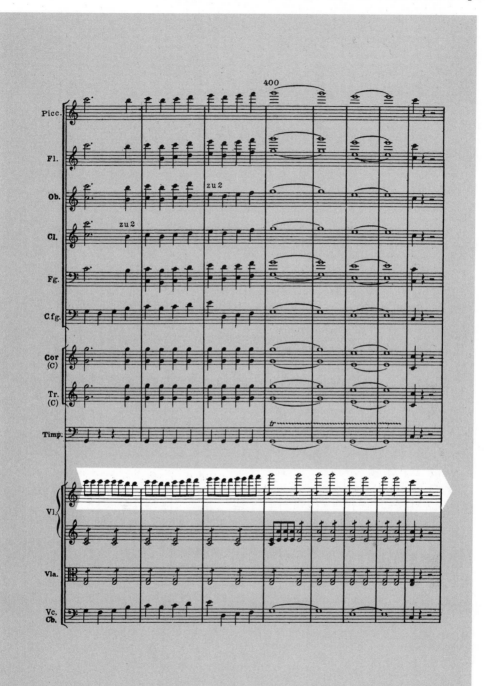

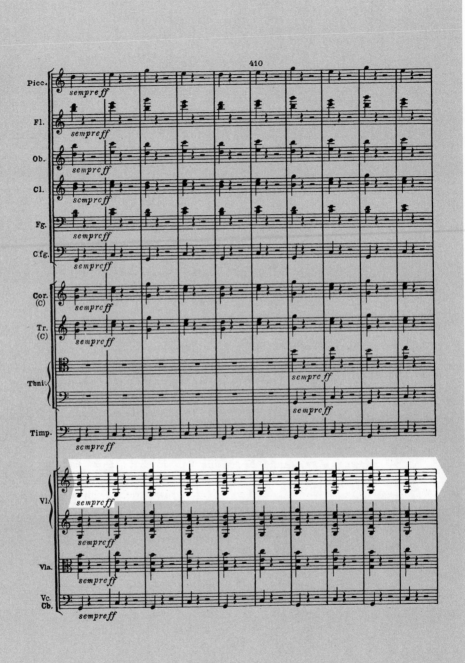

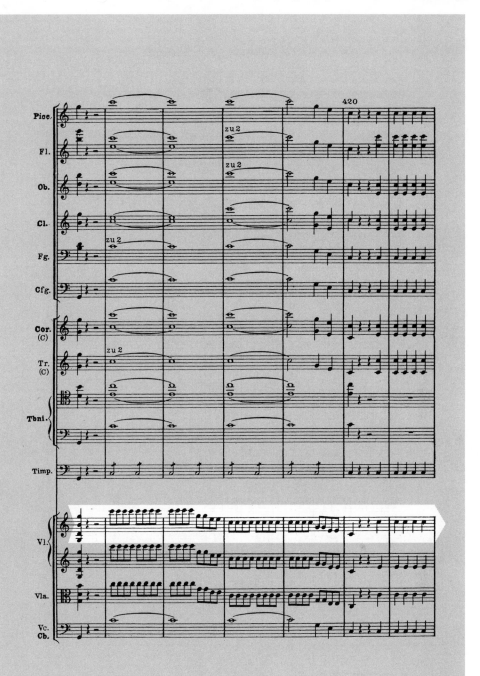

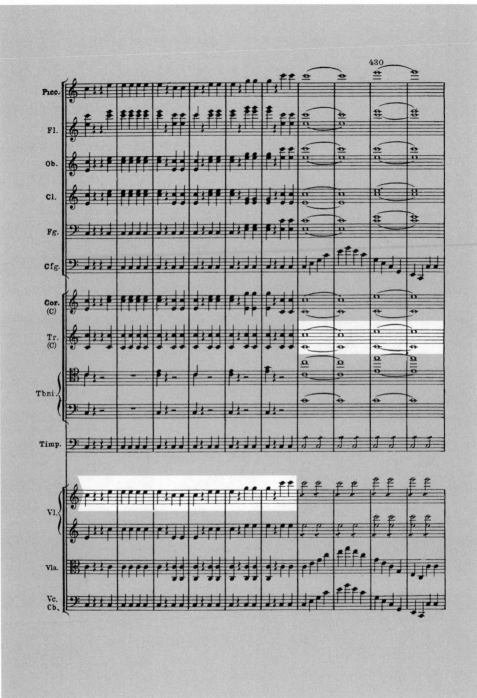

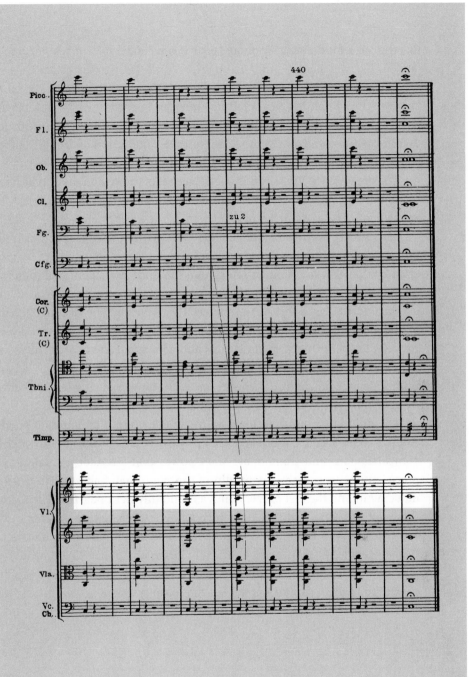

Beethoven's landmark symphony provides a model for concise, dramatic, and unified musical expression. In this work, Beethoven establishes the basic techniques of creating cyclic unity. Rather than treating each movement in the symphony as a separate entity, as in earlier works of the genre, Beethoven links them together with a common motive, a transition between the third and fourth movements, and a quotation of the third movement prior to the recapitulation in the fourth movement.

The four-note motive sounded at the outset of the symphony can be heard in all four movements. It is the principal motive of the sonata-allegro first movement. The radiant second movement, a loose theme-and-variations structure, features two thematic ideas. The rhythmic motive can most readily be heard in the second idea, especially on its repetition where it is emphasized by the brass and timpani. Although the third movement maintains the basic ternary **A-B-A** structure, triple meter, and quick tempo associated with a scherzo, the treatment of the material is unusual. The opening scherzo abandons the expected binary form for a simple alternation of two ideas: a mysterious theme in the lower strings and a forceful statement of the principal rhythmic motive in the horns. Surprisingly, the return of the scherzo brings a complete change of character, as Beethoven quietly leads us into a transition.

The dramatic crescendo into the finale ushers in a triumphant theme. Adding to the weight of this moment is the first appearance of the piccolo, contrabassoon, and trombones. Such power and force for a finale is unprecedented. Previously, the weight of the symphony had been on the first movement, and the last movement was generally light hearted. The second theme of the sonata-allegro structure features repeated statements of the four-note motive in diminution over a simple accompaniment motive. In the development, this accompaniment emerges as a powerful force and propels the movement into a quotation of the third movement, a repeat of the transition, and an exultant arrival at the recapitulation.

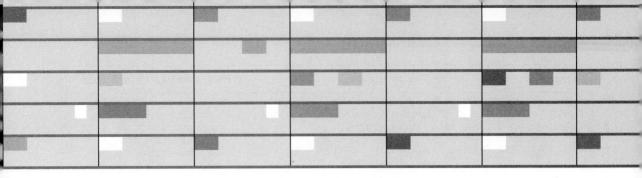

Appendix A

Reading a Musical Score

CLEFS

The music for some instruments is written in clefs other than the familiar treble and bass. In the following example, middle C is shown in the four clefs used in orchestral scores:

The *alto clef* is primarily used in viola parts. The *tenor clef* is employed for cello, bassoon, and trombone parts when these instruments play in a high register.

TRANSPOSING INSTRUMENTS

The music for some instruments is customarily written at a pitch different from its actual sound. The following list, with examples, shows the main transposing instruments and the degree of transposition. (In some modern works—such as the Stravinsky example included in volume two of this anthology—all instruments are written at their sounding pitch.)

Instrument	Transposition	Written note	Actual sound
Piccolo Celesta	sounds an octave higher than written		
Trumpet in F	sounds a fourth higher than written		
Trumpet in E	sounds a major third higher than written		
Clarinet in E♭ Trumpet in E♭	sounds a minor third higher than written		
Trumpet in D Clarinet in D	sounds a major second higher than written		
Clarinet in B♭ Trumpet in B♭ Cornet in B♭ French horn in B♭, alto	sounds a major second lower than written		
Clarinet in A Trumpet in A Cornet in A	sounds a minor third lower than written		
French horn in G Alto flute	sounds a fourth lower than written		
English horn French horn in F	sounds a fifth lower than written		
French horn in E	sounds a minor sixth lower than written		
French horn in E♭ Alto saxophone	sounds a major sixth lower than written		
French horn in D	sounds a minor seventh lower than written		
Contrabassoon French horn in C Double bass	sounds an octave lower than written		
Bass clarinet in B♭ Tenor saxophone (written in treble clef)	sounds a major ninth lower than written		
Tenor saxophone (written in bass clef)	sounds a major second lower than written		
Bass clarinet in A (written in treble clef)	sounds a minor tenth lower than written		
Bass clarinet in A (written in bass clef)	sounds a minor third lower than written		
Baritone saxophone in B♭ (written in treble clef)	sounds an octave and a major sixth lower than written		

Appendix B

Instrumental Names and Abbreviations

The following tables set forth the English, Italian, German, and French names used for the various musical instruments in these scores, and their respective abbreviations (when used). Latin voice designations and a table of the foreign-language names for scale degrees and modes are also provided.

English	*Italian*	*German*	*French*
WOODWINDS			
Piccolo (Picc.)	Flauto piccolo (Fl. Picc.)	Kleine Flöte (Kl. Fl.)	Petite flûte
Flute (Fl.)	Flauto (Fl.); Flauto grande (Fl. gr.)	Grosse Flöte (Gr. Fl.)	Flûte (Fl.)
Alto flute	Flauto contralto (fl. c-alto)	Altflöte	Flûte en sol
Oboe (Ob.)	Oboe (Ob.)	Hoboe (Hb.); Oboe (Ob.)	Hautbois (Hb.)
English horn (E. H.)	Corno inglese (C. or Cor. ingl., C.i.)	Englisches Horn (E. H.)	Cor anglais (C. A.)
E♭ clarinet	Clarinetto piccolo (clar. picc.)		

English	Italian	German	French
Clarinet (C., Cl., Clt., Clar.)	Clarinetto (Cl., Clar.)	Klarinette (Kl.)	Clarinette (Cl.)
Bass clarinet (B. Cl.)	Clarinetto basso (Cl. b., Cl. basso, Clar. basso)	Bass Klarinette (Bkl.)	Clarinette basse (Cl. bs.)
Bassoon (Bsn., Bssn.)	Fagotto (Fag., Fg.)	Fagott (Fag., Fg.)	Basson (Bssn.)
Contrabassoon (C. Bsn.)	Contrafagotto (Cfg., C. Fag., Cont. F.)	Kontrafagott (Kfg.)	Contrebasson (C. bssn.)
Alto saxophone Tenor saxophone Baritone saxophone	Sassofone	Saxophon	Saxophone
		BRASS	
French horn (Hr., Hn.)	Corno (Cor., C.)	Horn (Hr.) [pl. Hörner (Hrn.)]	Cor; Cor à pistons
Trumpet (Tpt., Trpt., Trp., Tr.)	Tromba (Tr.) [pl. Tbe.]	Trompete (Tr., Trp.)	Trompette (Tr.)
Trumpet in D	Tromba piccola (Tr. picc.)		
Cornet	Cornetta	Kornett	Cornet à pistons (C. à p., Pist.)
Trombone (Tr., Tbe., Trb., Trm., Trbe.)	Trombone [pl. Tromboni (Tbni., Trni.)]	Posaune (Ps., Pos.)	Trombone (Tr.)
Bass trombone Tuba (Tb.)	Tuba (Tb., Tba.)	Tuba (Tb.) [also Basstuba (Btb.)]	Tuba (Tb.)
Ophicleide	Oficleide	Ophikleide	Ophicléide
		PERCUSSION	
Percussion (Perc.)	Percussione	Schlagzeug (Schlag.)	Batterie (Batt.)
Kettledrums (K. D.)	Timpani (Timp., Tp.)	Pauken (Pk.)	Timbales (Timb.)
Snare drum (S. D.)	Tamburo piccolo (Tamb. picc.) Tamburo militare (Tamb. milit.)	Kleine Trommel (Kl. Tr.)	Caisse claire (C. cl.); Caisse roulante Tambour militaire (Tamb. milit.)
Bass drum (B. drum)	Gran cassa (Gr. Cassa, Gr. C., G. C.); Tamburo grande (T. gr.)	Grosse Trommel (Gr. Tr.)	Grosse caisse (Gr. c.)
Cymbals (Cym., Cymb.)	Piatti (P., Ptti., Piat.)	Becken (Beck.)	Cymbales (Cym.)
Tam-Tam (Tam.-T.)			
Tambourine (Tamb.)	Tamburino (Tamb.)	Schellentrommel; Tamburin	Tambour de Basque (T. de B., Tamb. de Basque)

English	Italian	German	French
Triangle (Trgl., Tri.)	Triangolo (Trgl.)	Triangel	Triangle (Triang.)
Glockenspiel (Glocken.)	Campanelli (Cmp.)	Glockenspiel	Carillon
Bells; Chimes	Campane (Cmp.)	Glocken	Cloches
Antique cymbals	Crotali; Piatti antichi	Antike Zimbeln	Crotales; Cymbales antiques
Sleigh bells	Sonagli (Son.)	Schellen	Grelots
Xylophone (Xyl.)	Xilofono	Xylophon	Xylophone
Cowbells		Herdenglocken	
Crash cymbal			Grande cymbale chinoise
Siren			Sirène
Lion's roar			Tambour à corde
Slapstick			Fouet
Wood blocks			Blocs chinois

STRINGS

English	Italian	German	French
Violin (V., Vl., Vln., Vi., Vn.)	Violino (V., Vl., Vln.)	Violine (V., Vl., Vln.); Geige (Gg.)	Violon (V., Vl., Vln.)
Viola (Va., Vl.) [pl. Vas.]	Viola (Va., Vla.) [pl. Viole (Vle.)]	Bratsche (Br.)	Alto (A.)
Violoncello; Cello (Vcl., Vc.)	Violoncello (Vc., Vlc., Vcllo.)	Violoncell (Vc., Vlc.)	Violoncelle (Vc.)
Double bass (D. Bs.)	Contrabasso (Cb., C. B.) [pl. Contrabassi or Bassi (C. Bassi, Bi.)]	Kontrabass (Kb.)	Contrebasse (C. B.)

OTHER INSTRUMENTS

English	Italian	German	French
Harp (Hp., Hrp.)	Arpa (A., Arp.)	Harfe (Hrf.)	Harpe (Hp.)
Piano	Pianoforte (P.-f., Pft.)	Klavier	Piano
Celesta (Cel.)			
Harpsichord	Cembalo	Cembalo	Clavecin
Fortepiano (Fp.)	Fortepiano		
Harmonium (Harmon.)			
Organ (Org.)	Organo	Orgel	Orgue
Guitar	Chitarra	Gitarre (Git.)	Guitare
Mandoline (Mand.)			
Continuous bass, thorough bass (cont.)	Basso continuo (B.C.)	Generalbass	Basse continue

Voice Designations

English	Latin	Italian
Soprano (S.), Treble	Cantus (C.), Superius	Canto
Alto (A.)	Altus, Contratenor	Alto, Contratenore
Tenor (T.)	Tenor	Tenore
Bass (B.)	Bassus, Contratenor Bassus	Basso
Fifth voice	Quintus (V, 5)	Quinto
Sixth voice	Sextus (VI, 6)	Sexto

Tenor: lowest voice in medieval polyphony
Triplum: third voice above Tenor in medieval polyphony
Duplum: second voice above Tenor in medieval polyphony

Names of Scale Degrees and Modes

English	Italian	German	French
SCALE DEGREES			
C	do	C	ut
C-sharp	do diesis	Cis	ut dièse
D-flat	re bemolle	Des	ré bémol
D	re	D	ré
D-sharp	re diesis	Dis	ré dièse
E-flat	mi bemolle	Es	mi bémol
E	mi	E	mi
E-sharp	mi diesis	Eis	mi dièse
F-flat	fa bemolle	Fes	fa bémol
F	fa	F	fa
F-sharp	fa diesis	Fis	fa dièse
G-flat	sol bemolle	Ges	sol bémol
G	sol	G	sol
G-sharp	sol diesis	Gis	sol dièse
A-flat	la bemolle	As	la bémol
A	la	A	la
A-sharp	la diesis	Ais	la dièse
B-flat	si bemolle	B	si bémol
B	si	H	si
B-sharp	si diesis	His	si dièse
C-flat	do bemolle	Ces	ut bémol
MODES			
major	maggiore	dur	majeur
minor	minore	moll	mineur

Medieval and Renaissance Instruments Heard in Norton Recordings

Strings, bowed	Winds
rebec	cornetto
vielle	3-hole pipe
viola da gamba	recorder
	sackbut
Strings, plucked	shawm
harp	
lute	Percussion
psaltery	tabor
Strings, struck	Keyboard
dulcimer	harpsichord
	organ

A Note on Baroque Instruments

In the Baroque era, certain instruments that are not used in today's modern orchestra were required by the composers; the following list defines these terms.

Continuo (Cont. or B.C.): A method of indicating an accompanying part by the bass notes only, together with figures (numbers) designating the chords to be played above them (figured bass). In general practice, the chords are played on a harpsichord or organ, while a viola da gamba or cello doubles the bass notes.

Oboe d'amore: In Bach's Cantata No. 80, this term indicates an alto oboe.

Ripieno (Rip.): Tutti, the full ensemble that alternates with the solo instrument or solo group (*Concertino*).

Taille (Tail.): In Bach's Cantata No. 80, this term indicates a tenor oboe or English horn.

Violino piccolo: A small violin, tuned a fourth higher than the standard violin.

Violone (V.): A string instrument intermediate in size between the cello and the double bass. (In modern performances, the double bass is commonly substituted.)

Appendix C

Glossary of Musical Terms Used in the Scores

The following glossary is not intended to be a complete dictionary of musical terms, nor is knowledge of all these terms necessary to follow the scores in this book. However, as listeners gain experience in following scores, they will find it useful and interesting to understand the composer's directions with regard to tempo, dynamics, and methods of performance.

In most cases, compound terms have been broken down and defined separately, as they often recur in varying combinations. A few common foreign-language words are included in addition to the musical terms. Note that names and abbreviations for instruments and for scale degrees will be found in Appendix B.

a   The phrases *a 2, a 3* (etc.) indicate the number of parts to be played by 2, 3 (etc.) players; when a simple number (1, 2, etc.) is placed over a part, it indicates that only the first (second, etc.) player in that group should play.

aber   But.

a cappella   In the manner of the chapel, as in unaccompanied choral singing.

accelerando (accel.)   Growing faster.

accordato, accordez   Tune the instrument as specified.

adagio   Slow, leisurely.

affettuoso   With emotion.

affrettare (affrett.)   Hastening a little.

agitando, agitato   Agitated, excited.

al fine   "The end"; an indication to return to the start of a piece and to repeat it only to the point marked "fine."

alla breve   Indicates two beats to a measure, at a rather quick tempo.

allargando (*allarg.*)   Growing broader.

alla turca   In the Turkish style.

alle, *alles*   All, every, each.

allegretto   A moderately fast tempo (between *allegro* and *andante*).

allegro   A rapid tempo (between *allegretto* and *presto*).

allein   Alone, solo.

allmählich   Gradually (*allmählich wieder gleichmässig fliessend werden*, gradually becoming even-flowing again).

alta, *alto*, *altus* (*A*).   The deeper of the two main divisions of women's (or boys') voices.

am Steg   On the bridge (of a string instrument).

ancora   Again.

andante   A moderately slow tempo (between *adagio* and *allegretto*).

andantino   A moderately slow tempo.

Anfang   Beginning, initial.

anima   Spirit, animation.

animando   With increasing animation.

animant, *animato*, *animé*, *animez*   Animated.

aperto   Indicates open notes on the horn, open strings, and undampened piano notes.

a piacere   The execution of the passage is left to the performer's discretion.

appassionato   Impassioned.

appena   Scarcely, hardly.

apprensivo   Apprehensive.

archet   Bow.

archi, *arco*   Played with the bow.

arditamente   Boldly.

arpeggiando, *arpeggiato* (*arpegg.*)   Played in harp style; i.e., the notes of the chord played in quick succession rather than simultaneously.

assai   Very.

assez   Fairly, rather.

attacca   Begin what follows without pausing.

a tempo   At the original tempo.

auf dem   On the (as in *auf dem G*, on the G string).

Ausdruck   Expression.

ausdrucksvoll   With expression.

äusserst   Extreme, utmost.

avec   With.

bachetta, *bachetti*   Drumsticks (*bachetti di spugna*, sponge-headed drumsticks).

baguettes   Drumsticks (*baguettes de bois*, wooden drumsticks; *baguettes d'éponge*, sponge-headed drumsticks).

bass, *bassi*, *basso*, *bassus* (*B.*)   The lowest male voice.

basso seguente   The bottom voice of a Renaissance or early Baroque work, played by an organ or harpsichord in the manner of a basso continuo.

battere, *battuta*, *battuto* (*batt.*)   To beat.

Becken   Cymbals.

bedeutend bewegter   With significantly more movement.

beider Hände   With both hands.

ben   Very.

bewegt   Agitated.

bewegter   More agitated.

bisbigliando, *bispiglando* (*bis.*)   Whispering.

bis zum Schluss dieser Szene   To the end of this scene.

blasen   Blow.

Blech   Brass instruments.

Bogen (*bog.*)   Played with the bow.

bois   Woodwind.

bouché   Muted.

breit   Broadly.

breiter   More broadly.

brio   Spirit, vivacity.

Brustpositiv   A division of an organ normally based on 2' or 4' pitch.

cadenza (*cad.*, *cadenz.*)   An extended passage for solo instrument in free, improvisatory style.

calando (*cal.*)   Diminishing in volume and speed.

calma, *calmo*   Calm, calmly.

cantabile (cant.)   In a singing style.

cantando   In a singing manner.

canto   Voice (as in *col canto*, a direction for the accompaniment to follow the solo part in tempo and expression).

cantus   An older designation for the highest part in a vocal work.

cantus firmus   Fixed song; a preexistent melody used as the structural basis of a polyphonic composition.

capriccio   Capriciously, whimsically.

changez   Change (usually an instruction to retune a string or an instrument).

chiuso See *gestopft*.

chorale A congregational hymn in the German Lutheran Church; sometimes used as the basis for large-scale compositions.

chromatisch Chromatic.

circa (c.) About, approximately.

closed The second of two endings in a secular medieval work, usually cadencing on the final.

coda A concluding section extraneous to the form; a formal closing gesture.

col, colla, coll' With the.

colore Colored.

come prima, come sopra As at first, as previously.

commodo Comfortable, easy.

con With.

concertino The solo group in a Baroque concerto grosso.

corda String; for example, *seconda (2a) corda* is the second string (the A string on the violin).

corto Short, brief.

crescendo (cresc.) An increase in volume.

cuivré Played with a harsh, blaring tone.

da capo (D.C.) Repeat from the beginning.

dal segno (D.S.) Repeat from the sign.

Dämpfer (Dpf.) Mutes.

dazu In addition to that, for that purpose.

de, des, die Of, from.

début Beginning

deciso Determined, resolute.

decrescendo (decresc., decr.) A decreasing of volume.

dehors Outside.

delicatamente Delicately.

dem To the.

détaché With a broad, vigorous bow stroke, each note bowed singly.

deutlich Distinctly.

d'exécution Performance.

diminuendo, diminuer (dim., dimin.) A decreasing of volume.

distinto Distinct, clear.

divisés, divisi (div.) Divided; indicates that the instrumental group should be divided into two parts to play the passage in question.

dolce Sweetly and softly.

dolcemente Sweetly.

dolcissimo (dolciss.) Very sweetly.

Doppelgriff Double stop.

doux Sweetly.

drängend Pressing on.

dreifach Triple.

dreitaktig Three beats to a measure.

dur Major, as in *G dur* (G major).

durée Duration.

e, et And.

eilen To hurry.

ein One, a.

elegante Elegant, graceful.

energico Energetically.

espansione Expansion, broadening.

espressione With expression.

espressivo (espr., espress.) Expressively.

etwas Somewhat, rather.

expressif Expressively.

facile Simple.

fagotto Bassoon; an organ reed stop.

fin, fine End, close.

finale Final movement or section of a work.

finalis Pitch on which a melody ends in a church mode; the final pitch.

Flatterzunge, flutter tongue A special tonguing technique for wind instruments, producing a rapid, trill-like sound.

flebile Feeble, plaintive, mournful.

fliessend Flowing.

forte (f) Loud.

fortepiano (fp) Loud followed immediately by soft.

fortissimo (ff) Very loud (*fff* indicates a still louder dynamic).

forza Force.

forzando (f$_z$) Forced, strongly accented.

fou Frantic.

frappez To strike.

frei Freely.

freihäng., freihängendes Hanging freely. An indication to the percussionist to let the cymbals vibrate freely.

frisch Fresh, lively.

furioso Furiously.

ganz Entirely, altogether.

Ganzton Whole tone.

gedämpft (*ged.*)   Muted.
geheimnisvoll   Mysteriously.
geschlagen   Pulsating.
gestopft (*gest.*)   Stopping the notes of a horn; that is, the hand is placed in the bell of the horn to produce a muffled sound. Also *chiuso*.
geteilt (*get.*)   Divided; indicates that the instrumental group should be divided into two parts to play the passage in question.
getragen   Sustained.
gewöhnlich   As usual.
giocoso   Humorous.
giusto   Moderately.
glissando (*gliss.*)   Rapid scales produced by sliding the fingers over all the strings.
gradamente   Gradually.
grande   Large, great.
grandioso   Grandiose.
grave   Slow, solemn; deep, low.
grazioso   Gracefully.
grosser Auftakt   Big upbeat.
gut   Good, well.

Hälfte   Half.
Hauptzeitmass   Original tempo.
hervortreten   Prominent.
hoch   High, nobly.
Holz   Woodwinds.
Holzschlägel   Wooden drumstick.

im gleichen Rhythmus   In the same rhythm.
immer   Always.
in Oktaven   In octaves.
insensibilmente   Slightly, imperceptibly.
intensa   Intensely.
istesso tempo   Duration of beat remains unaltered despite meter change.

jeu   Playful.
jubilus   The extended melisma sung to the final syllable of the word "Alleluia," in the Alleluia of the Proper of the Mass.
jusqu'à   Until.

kadenzieren   To cadence.
klagend   Lamenting.
kleine   Little.
klingen   To sound.

komisch bedeutsam   Very humorously.
kurz   Short.

langsam   Slow.
langsamer   Slower.
languendo, langueur   Languor.
l'archet   See *archet*.
largamente   Broadly.
larghetto   Slightly faster than *largo*.
largo   A very slow tempo.
lasci, lassen   To abandon.
lebhaft   Lively.
lebhafter   Livelier.
legatissimo   A more forceful indication of *legato*.
legato   Performed without any perceptible interruption between notes.
légèrement, leggieramente   Lightly.
leggiero (*legg.*)   Light and graceful.
legno   The wood of the bow (*col legno gestrich*, played with the wood).
lent   Slow.
lentamente   Slowly.
lento   A slow tempo (between *andante* and *largo*).
l.h.   Abbreviation for "left hand."
ligature   A notational device that combines two or more notes in a single symbol.
liricamente   Lyrically.
loco   Indicates a return to the written pitch, following a passage played an octave higher or lower than written.
lontano   Distant.
Luftpause   Pause for breath.
lunga   Long, sustained.
lusingando   Caressing.

ma, mais   But.
maestoso   Majestic.
maggiore   Major mode.
marcatissimo (*marcatiss.*)   With very marked emphasis.
marcato (*marc.*)   Marked, with emphasis.
marschmässig, nicht eilen   Moderate-paced march, not rushed.
marziale   Military, martial, march-like.
mässig   Moderately.
mässiger   More moderately.
même   Same.
meno   Less.
mezza voce   Restrained, with half voice.
mezzo forte (*mf*)   Moderately loud.

mezzo piano (mp) Moderately soft.

mindestens At least.

minore Minor mode.

misterioso Mysterious.

misura Measured.

mit With.

moderatissimo A more forceful indication of *moderato*.

moderato, modéré At a moderate tempo.

moins Less.

molto Very, much.

mordenti Biting, pungent.

morendo Dying away.

mormorato Murmured.

mosso Rapid.

moto Motion.

mouvement (mouv., mouvt.) Tempo.

muta, mutano Change the tuning of the instrument as specified.

nach After.

naturalezza A natural, unaffected manner.

neuen New.

neume A notational sign used in chant to designate pitch.

nicht Not.

niente Nothing.

nimmt To take; to seize.

noch Still.

non Not.

nuovo New.

obere, oberer (ob.) Upper, leading.

Oberwerk Secondary division of the organ, with pipes behind the player.

oder langsamer Or slower.

offen Open.

ohne Without.

ondeggiante Undulating movement of the bow, which produces a tremolo effect.

open The first ending in a secular medieval piece, usually cadencing on a pitch other than the final.

ordinario (ord., ordin.) In the usual way (generally canceling an instruction to play using some special technique).

ossia An alternative (usually easier) version of a passage.

ôtez vite les sourdines Remove the mutes quickly.

ottoni Brass.

ouvert Open.

parte Part (*colla parte*, the accompaniment is to follow the soloist in tempo).

passionato Passionately.

pastourelle A genre of troubadour or trouvère song built on a debate between a shepherdess and a knight.

Paukenschlägel Timpani stick.

pavillons en l'air An indication to the player of a wind instrument to raise the bell of the instrument upward.

pedal, pedale (ped., P.) (1) In piano music, indicates that the damper pedal should be depressed; an asterisk indicates the point of release (brackets below the music are also used to indicate pedaling). (2) On an organ, the pedals are a keyboard played with the feet.

per During.

perdendosi Gradually dying away.

pesante Heavily.

peu Little, a little.

piacevole Agreeable, pleasant.

pianissimo (pp) Very soft (*ppp* indicates a still softer dynamic).

piano (p) Soft.

più More.

pizzicato (pizz.) The string plucked with the finger.

plötzlich Suddenly, immediately.

plus More.

pochissimo (pochiss.) Very little, a very little.

poco Little, a little.

ponticello (pont.) The bridge (of a string instrument).

portamento Continuous smooth and rapid sliding between two pitches.

position naturel (pos. nat.) In the normal position (usually canceling an instruction to play using some special technique).

possibile Possible.

premier mouvement (1er mouvt.) At the original tempo.

prenez Take up.

préparez Prepare.

presque Almost, nearly.

presser To press.

prestissimo A more forceful indication of *presto*.

presto   A very quick tempo (faster than *allegro*).

prima, *primo*   First, principal.

quarta   Fourth.

quasi   Almost, as if.

quinto   Fifth.

rallentando (*rall.*, *rallent.*)   Growing slower.

rapidamente   Quickly.

rapidissimo (*rapidiss.*)   Very quickly.

rasch   Quickly.

rascher   More quickly.

rauschend   Rustling, roaring.

recitative (*recit.*)   A vocal style designed to imitate and emphasize the natural inflections of speech.

refrain   Text or music that is repeated within a larger composition, especially in a fixed poetic form such as the rondeau, virelai, or ballade.

rein   Perfect interval.

reprise   Repeat; in French Baroque music, the second section of a binary form.

respiro   Pause for breath.

retenu   Held back.

r.h.   Abbreviation for "right hand."

richtig   Correct (*richtige Lage*, correct pitch).

rien   Nothing.

rigore di tempo   Strictness of tempo.

rinforzando (*rf.*, *rfz.*, *rinf.*)   A sudden accent on a single note or chord.

ripieno   Tutti; in a Baroque concerto grosso, the whole ensemble.

ritardando (*rit.*, *ritard.*)   Gradually slackening in speed.

ritenuto (*riten.*)   Immediate reduction of speed.

ritmato   Rhythmic.

ritornando, *ritornello* (*ritor.*)   Refrain.

rubato   A certain elasticity and flexibility of tempo, consisting of slight accelerandos and ritardandos according to the requirements of the musical expression.

Rückpositiv   Secondary division of an organ, with pipes behind the player.

ruhig   Quietly.

sans   Without.

Schalltrichter   Horn.

scherzando (*scherz.*)   Playful.

schlagen   To strike in a usual manner.

Schlagwerk   Striking mechanism.

schleppen, *schleppend*   Dragging.

Schluss   Cadence, conclusion.

schnell   Fast.

schneller   Faster.

schon   Already.

Schwammschlägeln   Sponge-headed drumstick.

scorrevole   Flowing, gliding.

sec, *secco*   Dry, simple.

secundà   Second.

segue   Following immediately.

sehr   Very.

semplicità   Simplicity.

sempre   Always, continually.

senza   Without.

sesquialtera   Organ stop of two ranks, which sounds the twelfth and the seventeenth.

sforzando (*sf.*, *sfz.*)   With sudden emphasis.

simile (*sim.*)   In a similar manner.

sin   Without.

Singstimme   Singing voice.

sino al   Up to the . . . (usually followed by a new tempo marking, or by a dotted line indicating a terminal point).

si piace   Especially pleasing.

smorzando (*smorz.*)   Dying away.

sofort   Immediately.

soli, *solo* (*s.*)   Executed by one performer.

sopra   Above; in piano music, used to indicate that one hand must pass above the other.

soprano (*S.*)   The voice classification with the highest range.

sordini, *sordino* (*sord.*)   Mute.

sostenendo, *sostenuto* (*sost.*)   Sustained.

sotto voce   In an undertone, subdued, under the breath.

sourdine (*sourd.*)   Mute.

soutenu   Sustained.

spiel, *spielen*   Play (an instrument).

Spieler   Player, performer.

spirito   Spirit, soul.

spiritoso   In a spirited manner.

spugna   Sponge.

staccato (*stacc.*)   Detached, separated, abruptly, disconnected.

stentando, *stentare*, *stentato* (*stent.*)   Delaying, retarding.

stesso The same.

stile concitato Agitated style, devised by Monteverdi, involving rapid reiterations of a single pitch.

Stimme Voice.

stimmen To tune.

strappato Bowing indication for pulled, or long, strokes.

strascinare To drag.

Streichinstrumente (*Streichinstr.*) Bowed string instruments.

strepitoso Noisy, loud.

stretto In a nonfugal composition, indicates a concluding section at an increased speed.

stringendo (*string.*) Quickening.

subito (*sub.*) Suddenly, immediately.

sul On the (as in *sul G*, on the G string).

superius In older music, the uppermost part.

sur On.

tacet The instrument or vocal part so marked is silent.

tasto solo In a continuo part, this indicates that only the string instrument plays; the chord-playing instrument is silent.

tempo primo (*tempo I*) At the original tempo.

teneramente, tenero Tenderly, gently.

tenor, tenore (*T.*) The highest male voice; the structural voice in early music.

tenuto (*ten., tenu.*) Held, sustained.

tertia Third.

tief Deep, low.

touche Key; note.

toujours Always, continually.

tranquillo Quietly, calmly.

tre corde (*t.c.*) Release the soft (or *una corda*) pedal of the piano.

tremolo (*trem.*) On string instruments, a quick reiteration of the same tone, produced by a rapid up-and-down movement of the bow; also a rapid alternation between two different notes.

très Very.

trill (*tr.*) The rapid alternation of a given note with the diatonic second above it. In a drum part, it indicates rapid alternating strokes with two drumsticks.

Trommschlag (*Tromm.*) Drumbeat.

troppo Too much.

tutta la forza Very emphatically.

tutti Literally, "all"; usually means all the instruments in a given category as distinct from a solo part.

übergreifen To overlap.

übertonend Drowning out.

umstimmen To change the tuning.

un One, a.

una corda (*u.c.*) With the "soft" pedal of the piano depressed.

und And.

unison (*unis.*) The same notes or melody played by several instruments at the same pitch. Often used to emphasize that a phrase is not to be divided among several players.

unmerklich Imperceptible.

velocissimo Very swiftly.

verklingen lassen To let die away.

verse A group of lines in a poem, sometimes separated by a recurring refrain; also small units of text from the Bible, sung as a solo in alternation with a choral response.

vibrare To sound.

vibrato (*vibr.*) To fluctuate the pitch on a single note.

vierfach Quadruple.

vierhändig Four-hand piano music.

vif Lively.

vigoroso Vigorous, strong.

vivace Quick, lively.

vivacissimo A more forceful indication of *vivace*.

vivente, vivo Lively.

voce Voice (as in *colla voce*, a direction for the accompaniment to follow the solo part in tempo and expression).

volles Orch. Entire orchestra.

Vorhang auf Curtain up.

Vorhang zu Curtain down.

vorher Beforehand, previously.

voriges Preceding.

Waltzertempo In the tempo of a waltz.

weg Away, beyond.

weich Mellow, smooth, soft.

wie aus der Fern As if from afar.

wieder   Again.

wie zu Anfang dieser Szene   As at the beginning of this scene.

zart   Tenderly, delicately.

Zeit   Time; duration.

zögernd   Slower.

zu   The phrases *zu 2, zu 3* (etc.) indicate the number of parts to be played by 2, 3 (etc.) players.

zum   In addition.

zurückhaltend   Slackening in speed.

zurücktreten   To withdraw.

zweihändig   With two hands.

Appendix D

Concordance Table for Recordings and Listening Guides

The following table provides cross-references to the Listening Guides (LG) in *The Enjoyment of Music*, Ninth Edition, by Joseph Machlis and Kristine Forney (New York: Norton, 2003). The following abbreviations are used throughout: *Chr* for the Chronological version, *Std* for the Standard version, and *Sh* for the Shorter version. The table also gives the location of each work on both recording sets (see "A Note on the Recordings," p. xiv).

Chr LG #	Std LG #	Sh LG #	Score Number, Composer, Title	Score Page	8-CD Set	4-CD Set
1	1	1	Britten, *Young Person's Guide to the Orchestra* (score not included)	—	(Student Resource CD)	
2	34	—	1. Gregorian Chant: *Kyrie*	1	1/1–3	—
3	35	2	2. Hildegard of Bingen: *Alleluia, O virga mediatrix* (*Alleluia, O mediating branch*)	3	1/4–6	1/1–3
4	36	3	3. Notre Dame School Organum: *Gaude Maria virgo* (*Rejoice Mary, virgin*)	8	1/7–8	1/4–5
5	37	—	4. Adam de la Halle, Motet: *Aucun se sont loé/A Dieu/Super te* (*There are those who praise/To God/Above you*)	10	1/9–10	—
6	38	—	5. Moniot d'Arras: *Ce fut en mai* (*It happened in May*)	14	1/11–15	—
7	39	4	6. Machaut: *Puis qu'en oubli* (*Since I am forgotten*)	18	1/16–20	1/6–10
8	40	—	7. Anonymous: *Royal estampie* No. 4	20	1/21–27	—

CHR LG #	STD LG #	SH LG #	SCORE NUMBER, COMPOSER, TITLE	SCORE PAGE	8-CD SET	4-CD SET
9	41	—	8. ANONYMOUS: *L'homme armé* tune DU FAY: *L'homme armé* Mass (*The Armed Man Mass*), Kyrie	22	1/28–31	—
10	42	5	9. JOSQUIN: *Ave Maria . . . virgo serena (Hail Mary . . . gentle virgin)*	29	1/32–38	1/11–17
12	44	—	10. JOSQUIN: *Mille regretz (A thousand regrets)*	38	1/39–40	—
13	45	—	11. SUSATO: Pavane *Mille regretz*	41	1/41–43	—
11	43	6	12. PALESTRINA: *Pope Marcellus* Mass, Gloria	43	1/44–45	1/18–19
16	48	—	13. GIOVANNI GABRIELI: *O quam suavis (O how sweet)*	51	1/46–47	—
14	46	—	14. MONTEVERDI: *A un giro sol (At a single turning glance)*	61	1/48–50	—
17	49	—	15. MONTEVERDI: *L'incoronazione di Poppea (The Coronation of Poppea)*, Act III, Scene 7	67	1/51–55	—
15	47	7	16. FARMER: *Fair Phyllis*	77	1/56	1/20
19	51	9	17. STROZZI: *Begli occhi (Beautiful Eyes)*	82	1/57–62	1/24–29
22	54	—	18. CORELLI: Trio Sonata, Op. 3, No. 2, in D major Third movement Fourth movement	90 91	1/63 1/64–65	— —
18	50	8	19. PURCELL: *Dido and Aeneas*, Act III, Dido's Lament	94	1/66–68	1/21–23
23	55	12	20. VIVALDI: *La primavera*, from *Le Quattro stagioni* (*Spring*, from *The Four Seasons*) First movement Second movement Third movement	98 109 113	1/69–74 1/75 1/76	1/45–50 — —
25	57	13	21. HANDEL: *Water Music*, Suite in D major Allegro Alla hornpipe	128 133	2/1–3 2/4–6	— 1/51–53
21	53	11	22. HANDEL: *Messiah* No. 1, Overture No. 14, "There were shepherds" No. 17, "Glory to God" No. 18, "Rejoice greatly" No. 44, "Hallelujah"	140 146 148 153 159	2/7–8 2/9–11 2/12 2/13–15 2/16–18	— — — 1/39–41 1/42–44
26	58	—	23. BACH: Chorale Prelude, *Ein feste Burg ist unser Gott (A Mighty Fortress Is Our God)*	170	2/19–26	—
24	56	—	24. BACH: *Brandenburg Concerto* No. 2 in F major First movement Second movement	175 195	2/27–31 2/32	— —
27	59	14	25. BACH: Prelude and Fugue in C minor, from *The Well-Tempered Clavier*, Book I	199	2/33–38	1/54–59
20	52	10	26. BACH: Cantata No. 80, *Ein feste Burg ist unser Gott (A Mighty Fortress Is Our God)* No. 1, Choral fugue No. 2, Duet No. 5, Chorus No. 8, Chorale	204 231 239 257	2/39–45 2/46–47 2/48–49 2/50–51	1/30–36 — — 1/37–38

CHR LG #	STD LG #	SH LG #	SCORE NUMBER, COMPOSER, TITLE	SCORE PAGE	8-CD SET	4-CD SET
28	60	—	27. GAY: *The Beggar's Opera*, end of Act II	260	2/52–54	—
32	25	16	28. HAYDN: Symphony No. 94 in G major (*Surprise*), second movement	265	2/55–61	2/1–7
29	22	—	29. HAYDN: String Quartet in D minor, Op. 76, No. 2 (*Quinten*), fourth movement	278	2/62–67	—
38	31	—	30. HAYDN: *Die Schöpfung (The Creation)*, Part I,		3/1–3	—
			No. 12, Recitative, "Und Gott sprach, Es sei'n Lichter"	287	3/1	—
			No. 13, Recitative, "In vollem Glanze"	288	3/2	—
			No. 14, Chorus, "Die Himmel erzählen"	290	3/3	—
36	29	—	31. MOZART: Piano Sonata in A major, K. 331, third movement	304	3/4–10	—
34	27	18	32. MOZART: Piano Concerto in G major, K. 453			
			First movement	309	3/11–21	2/33–43
			Second movement	341	3/22–27	—
			Third movement	352	3/28–34	—
39	32	20	33. MOZART: *Le nozze di Figaro (The Marriage of Figaro)*			
			Overture	378	3/35–39	—
			Act I, Scenes 6 and 7	400	3/40–47	2/49–56
30	23	15	34. MOZART: *Eine kleine Nachtmusik*, K. 525			
			First movement	433	3/48–52	1/60–64
			Second movement	440	3/53–58	1/65–70
			Third movement	445	3/59–61	1/71–73
			Fourth movement	446	3/62–67	1/74–79
31	24	—	35. MOZART: Symphony No. 40 in G minor, K. 550, first movement	456	4/1–5	—
37	30	19	36. BEETHOVEN: Piano Sonata in C minor, Op. 13 (*Pathétique*)			
			First movement	483	4/6–11	—
			Second movement	490	4/12–16	2/44–48
			Third movement	493	4/17–23	—
35	28	—	37. BEETHOVEN: Violin Concerto in D major, Op. 61, third movement	500	4/24–31	—
33	26	17	38. BEETHOVEN: Symphony No. 5 in C minor, Op. 67			
			First movement	524	4/32–37	2/8–13
			Second movement	554	4/38–44	2/14–20
			Third movement	575	4/45–48	2/21–24
			Fourth movement	594	4/49–56	2/25–32

Acknowledgements

Page 3: Hildegard von Bingen, *Alleluia, O virga mediatrix.* © Otto Müller Verlag, Salzburg, 1992. **Page 5:** Hildegard von Bingen, *Alleluia, O virga mediatrix.* Reprinted with permission of Hildegard Publishing Company. **Page 8:** Notre Dame School, *Gaude Maria virgo.* Editions de L'Oiseau-Lyre S.A.M., Monaco 1993. **Page 10:** Adam de la Halle, *Aucun se sont loé/A Dieu/Super te.* Reprinted with permission of American Institute of Musicology. **Page 14:** Moniot d'Arras, *Ce fut en mai.* Reprinted by permission of Bärenreiter Music Corporation. **Page 18:** Guillaume de Machaut, *Puis qu'en oubli.* Editions de L'Oiseau-Lyre S.A.M., Monaco 1974. **Page 20:** Anonymous, *Royal estampie* No. 4. Edited by Timothy McGee. Reprinted with permission of Indiana University Press. **Page 22:** Guillaume Du Fay, *L'homme armé* Mass. Edited by Alejandro Planchart. Used by permission. **Page 29:** Josquin des Prez, *Ave Maria . . . virgo serena.* Edited by Alejandro Planchart. Used by permission. **Page 38:** Josquin des Prez, *Mille regretz.* Reprinted by permission of the publisher from "Mille Regretz" in *The Chanson and Madrigal,* edited by James Haar, pp. 143–46, Cambridge, Mass.: Harvard University Press, Copyright © 1964 by the President and Fellows of Harvard College. **Page 43:** Giovanni Pierluigi da Palestrina, *Pope Marcellus* Mass. Reprinted with permission of Istituto Italiano per la Storia della Musica. **Page 51:** Giovanni Gabrieli, *O quam suavis.* Reprinted with permission of American Institute of Musicology. **Page 61:** Claudio Monteverdi, *A un giro sol.* Reprinted with permission of Fondazione Claudio Monteverdi. **Page 67:** Claudio Monteverdi, *L'incoronazione di Poppea.* Music attributed to Claudio Monteverdi and Francesco Sacrati. Text by Giovanni Francesco Busenello. Edited by Alan Curtis. Copyright © 1989 by Novello & Company Limited, 8/9 Frith Street, London W1D 3UB, England. International Copyright Secured. All Rights Reserved. Reprinted by Permission. **Page 77:** John Farmer, *Fair Phyllis.* Score and lyrics to *Fair Phyllis* by John Farmer (pp. 54–57) from *The Penguin Book of Madrigals for Four Voices,* edited by Denis Stevens (Penguin Books, 1967) copyright © Denis

Stevens, 1967. **Page 82:** Barbara Strozzi, *Begli occhi.* Pp. 43–49 in *Cantate, Ariete a una, due e tre voci, Opus 3,* edited by Gail Archer, *Recent Researches in Music of the Baroque Era,* vol. 83. Madison, WI: A-R Editions, Inc., 1997. **Page 90:** Arcangelo Corelli, Trio Sonata, Op. 3, No. 2. Reprinted with permission of American Institute of Musicology. **Page 98:** Antonio Vivaldi, *La primavera* from *Le Quattro stagioni.* Edited by Simon Launchbury. © 1982 Ernst Eulenburg Ltd. Revised edition © 1996 Ernst Eulenburg Ltd. All Rights Reserved. Used by permission of European American Music Distributors LLC, sole U.S. and Canadian agent for Ernst Eulenburg & Co. GmbH. **Page 140:** George Frideric Handel, *Messiah.* Music by George F. Handel. Edited and arranged by Harold Watkins Shaw. Copyright © 1959 (Renewed) by Novello & Company Limited, 8/9 Frith Street, London W1D 3UB, England. Copyright © renewed 1987. Revised Edition © 1992 by Novello & Company Limited. International Copyright Secured. All Rights Reserved. Reprinted by Permission. **Page 170:** Johann Sebastian Bach, Chorale Prelude, *Ein feste Burg ist unser Gott.* Reprinted by permission of Bärenreiter Music Corporation. **Page 175:** Johann Sebastian Bach, *Brandenburg Concerto* No. 2 in F major. Edited by Karin Stöckl. © 1984 Ernst Eulenburg & Co. GmbH. All Rights Reserved. Used by permission of European American Music Distributors LLC, sole U.S. and Canadian agent for Ernst Eulenburg & Co. GmbH. **Page 204:** Johann Sebastian Bach, Cantata No. 80, *Ein feste Burg ist unser Gott.* Used by kind permission of European American Music Distributors LLC, sole U.S. and Canadian agent for Ernst Eulenburg & Co. GmbH. **Page 260:** John Gay, *The Beggar's Opera. The Music of John Gay's "The Beggar's Opera."* Edited and arranged by Jeremy Barlow. © Oxford University Press 1990. Used by permission. All rights reserved. **Page 265:** Franz Joseph Haydn, Symphony No. 94 in G major. Edited by Harry Newstone. © 1984 Ernst Eulenburg Ltd. All Rights Reserved. Used by permission of European American Music Distributors LLC, sole U.S. and Canadian agent for Ernst Eulenburg & Co. GmbH. **Page 278:** Franz Joseph Haydn, String Quartet, Op. 76, No. 2. Used by kind permission of European American Music Distributors LLC, sole U.S. and Canadian agent for Ernst Eulenburg & Co. GmbH. **Page 287:** Franz Joseph Haydn, *Die Schöpfung.* Arranged by Vincent Novello. Copyright © 1951 (Renewed) by G. Schirmer, Inc. (ASCAP) International Copyright Secured, All Rights Reserved. Reprinted by Permission. **Page 309:** Wolfgang Amadeus Mozart, Piano Concerto in G major, K. 453. Reprinted by permission of Bärenreiter Music Corporation. **Page 378:** Wolfgang Amadeus Mozart, *Le nozze di Figaro,* Overture. Used by kind permission of European American Music Distributors LLC, sole U.S. and Canadian agent for Ernst Eulenburg & Co. GmbH. **Page 400:** Wolfgang Amadeus Mozart, *Le nozze di*

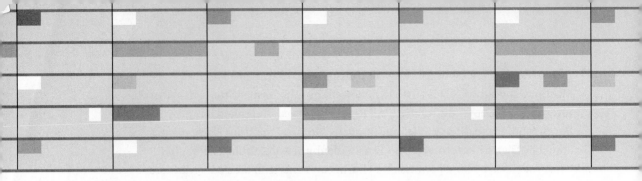

Index of Forms and Genres

A roman numeral following a title indicates a movement within the work named.

A-B-A form: *see* ternary form
A-B form: *see* binary form
air:
  GAY, *The Beggar's Opera*, Nos. 38–40 (p. 260)
Alleluia:
  HILDEGARD VON BINGEN, *Alleluia, O virga mediatrix* (p. 3)
aria: *see also* da capo aria, air
  BACH, Cantata No. 80, II (p. 231)
  HANDEL, *Messiah*, "Rejoice greatly" (p. 153)
  MONTEVERDI, *L'incoronazione di Poppea*, "Pur ti miro" (p. 71)
  MOZART, *Le nozze di Figaro*, Act I, No. 6 (p. 400)
  PURCELL: *Dido and Aeneas*, Dido's Lament (p. 94)

basso ostinato: *see* ground bass
ballad opera:
  GAY, *The Beggar's Opera* (p. 260)
binary form: *see also* rounded binary form
  GAY, *The Beggar's Opera*, No. 40 (p. 260)

cadenza:
  MOZART, Piano Concerto in G major, K. 453, I (p. 309); II (p. 341); III (p. 352)
  BEETHOVEN, Violin Concerto in D major, Op. 61, III (p. 500)
cantata:
  BACH, Cantata No. 80 (p. 204)
  STROZZI, *Begli occhi* (p. 82)
cantus firmus:
  DU FAY, *L'homme armé* Mass (p. 22)
chaconne: *see* ground bass
chamber music:
  CORELLI, Trio Sonata, Op. 3, No. 2 (p. 90)
  HAYDN, String Quartet in D minor, Op. 76, No. 2 (*Quinten*) (p. 278)
  MOZART, *Eine kleine Nachtmusik* (p. 433)
chanson:
  JOSQUIN, *Mille regretz* (p. 38)
  MACHAUT, *Puis qu'en oubli* (p. 18)
  MONIOT D'ARRAS, *Ce fut en mai* (p. 14)
chant:
  ADAM DE LA HALLE, Motet, *Aucun se sont loé / A Dieu / Super te* (p. 10)

GREGORIAN CHANT, Kyrie (p. 1)

HILDEGARD VON BINGEN, *Alleluia, O virga mediatrix* (p. 3)

ORGANUM, *Gaude Maria virgo* (p. 8)

choral music:

BACH, Cantata No. 80, I (p. 204); V (p. 239); VIII (p. 257)

ADAM DE LA HALLE, Motet, *Aucun se sont loé/A Dieu/Super te* (p. 10)

DU FAY, *L'homme armé* Mass (p. 22)

FARMER, *Fair Phyllis* (p. 77)

GABRIELI, *O quam suavis* (p. 51)

GREGORIAN CHANT, Kyrie (p. 1)

HANDEL, *Messiah*, "Glory to God in the highest" (p. 148); "Hallelujah" (p. 159)

HAYDN, *Die Schöpfung*, "Die Himmel erzählen" (p. 290)

HILDEGARD VON BINGEN, *Alleluia, O virga mediatrix* (p. 3)

JOSQUIN, *Ave Maria . . . virgo serena* (p. 29); *Mille regretz* (p. 38)

MONTEVERDI, *A un giro sol* (p. 61); *L'incoronazione di Poppea*, Act III, scene 7 (p. 67)

ORGANUM, *Gaude Maria virgo* (p. 8)

PALESTRINA, *Pope Marcellus* Mass, Gloria (p. 43)

chorale:

BACH, Cantata No. 80, I (p. 204); II (p. 231); V (p. 239); VIII (p. 257); Chorale prelude, *Ein feste Burg is unser Gott* (p. 170)

chorale cantata:

BACH, Cantata No. 80 (p. 204)

chorale prelude:

BACH, *Ein feste Burg ist unser Gott* (p. 170)

chorus from cantata:

BACH, Cantata No. 80, I (p. 204); V (p. 239); VIII (p. 257)

chorus from oratorio:

HANDEL, *Messiah*, "Glory to God" (p. 148); "Hallelujah" (p. 159)

HAYDN, *Die Schöpfung*, "Die Himmel erzählen" (p. 290)

concerto:

BACH, *Brandenburg Concerto* No. 2 in F major (p. 175)

BEETHOVEN, Violin Concerto in D major, Op. 61 (p. 500)

MOZART, Piano Concerto in G major, K. 453 (p. 309)

VIVALDI, *La primavera*, from *Le quattro stagioni* (p. 98)

concerto form: *see* first movement concerto form

continuous imitation:

BACH, Brandenburg Concerto No. 2 in F major, II (p. 195)

da capo aria (related forms):

HANDEL, *Messiah*, "Rejoice greatly" (p. 153)

MONTEVERDI, *L'incoronazione di Poppea*, "Pur ti miro" (p. 71)

dance music:

ANONYMOUS, *Royal estampie* No. 4 (p. 20)

HANDEL, *Water Music*, Suite in D major, Alla hornpipe (p. 133)

SUSATO, Pavane *Mille regretz* (p. 41)

double exposition form: *see* first movement concerto form

duet, vocal:

BACH, Cantata No. 80, II (p. 231)

MONTEVERDI, *L'incoronazione di Poppea*, "Pur ti miro" (p. 71)

STROZZI, *Begli occhi* (p. 82)

ensemble, opera:

MOZART, *Le nozze di Figaro*, Act I, No. 7 (p. 415)

estampie:

ANONYMOUS, *Royal estampie* No. 4 (p. 20)

first-movement concerto form:

MOZART, Piano Concerto in G major, K. 453, I (p. 309); II (p. 341)

French overture: *see* overture, French

fugue:

BACH, Cantata No. 80, I (p. 204)

BACH, Prelude and Fugue in C minor (p. 201)

Gloria:

PALESTRINA, *Pope Marcellus* Mass (p. 43)

ground bass (basso ostinato):

MONTEVERDI, *L'incoronazione di Poppea*, "Pur ti miro" (p. 71)

PURCELL, *Dido and Aeneas*, Dido's Lament (p. 94)

harpsichord music:

BACH, Prelude and Fugue in C minor (p. 199)

historical instruments:

ANONYMOUS, *Royal estampie* No. 4 (p. 20)

BACH, *Brandenburg Concerto* No. 2 in F major (p. 175)

MONIOT D'ARRAS, *Ce fut en mai* (p. 14)

GABRIELI, *O quam suavis* (p. 51)

HANDEL, *Messiah* (p. 140); *Water Music* (p. 128)

HAYDN, *Die Schöpfung* (p. 287); Symphony No. 94 in G major *(Surprise)* (p. 265)

MOZART, Piano Sonata in A major, K. 331 (p. 304)

SUSATO, Pavane *Mille regretz* (p. 41)

VIVALDI, *La primavera*, from *Le quattro stagioni* (p. 98)

hornpipe:

HANDEL, *Water Music*, Suite in D major, Alla hornpipe (p. 133)

instrumental music:

ANONYMOUS, *Royal estampie* No. 4 (p. 20)

BACH, *Brandenburg Concerto* No. 2 in F major (p. 175); Chorale prelude, *Ein feste Burg ist unser Gott* (p. 170)

BEETHOVEN, Piano Sonata in C minor, Op. 13 (*Pathétique*) (p. 483); Symphony No. 5 in C minor, Op. 67 (p. 524); Violin Concerto in D major, Op. 61 (p. 500)

CORELLI, Trio Sonata, Op. 3, No. 2 (p. 90)

HANDEL, *Messiah*, Overture (p. 140); *Water Music* (p. 128)

HAYDN, String Quartet in D minor, Op. 76, No. 2 (*Quinten*) (p. 278); Symphony No. 94 in G major (*Surprise*) (p. 265)

MONTEVERDI, *L'incoronazione di Poppea*, Act III, scene 7, Sinfonia (p. 67)

MOZART, *Eine kleine Nachtmusik* (p. 433); Piano Concerto in G major, K. 453 (p. 309); Piano Sonata in A major, K. 331 (p. 304); Symphony No. 40 in G minor (p. 456)

SUSATO, Pavane *Mille regretz* (p. 41)

VIVALDI, *La primavera*, from *Le quattro stagioni* (p. 98)

introduction, slow:

BEETHOVEN, Piano Sonata in C minor, Op. 13 (*Pathétique*) I (p. 483)

keyboard music:

BACH, Chorale prelude, *Ein feste Burg ist unser Gott* (p. 170); Prelude and Fugue in C minor (p. 199)

BEETHOVEN, Piano Sonata in C minor, Op. 13 (*Pathétique*) (p. 483)

MOZART, Piano Concerto in G major, K. 453 (p. 309); Piano Sonata in A major, K. 331 (p. 304)

Kyrie:

GREGORIAN CHANT, Kyrie (p. 1)

lament:

PURCELL, *Dido and Aeneas*, Dido's Lament (p. 94)

madrigal, English:

FARMER, *Fair Phyllis* (p. 77)

madrigal, Italian:

MONTEVERDI, *A un giro sol* (p. 61)

Mass movement:

DU FAY, *L'homme armé* Mass, Kyrie (p. 22)

GREGORIAN CHANT, Kyrie (p. 1)

HILDEGARD VON BINGEN, *Alleluia, O virga mediatrix* (p. 3)

PALESTRINA, *Pope Marcellus* Mass, Gloria (p. 43)

minuet and trio:

MOZART, *Eine kleine Nachtmusik*, III (p. 445)

motet:

ADAM DE LA HALLE, *Aucun se sont loé/A Dieu/Super te* (p. 10)

GABRIELI, *O quam suavis* (p. 51)

JOSQUIN, *Ave Maria . . . virgo serena* (p. 29)

non-Western influences:

MOZART, Piano Sonata in A major, K. 331, III (p. 304)

opera:

GAY, *The Beggar's Opera* (p. 260)

MONTEVERDI, *L'incoronazione di Poppea* (p. 67)

MOZART, *Le nozze di Figaro* (p. 378)

PURCELL, *Dido and Aeneas* (p. 94)

oratorio:

HANDEL, *Messiah* (p. 140)

HAYDN, *Die Schöpfung* (p. 287)

orchestral music:

BACH, *Brandenburg Concerto* No. 2 (p. 175)

BEETHOVEN, Symphony No. 5 in C minor, Op. 67 (p. 524); Violin Concerto in D major, Op. 61 (p. 500)

HANDEL, *Messiah*, Overture (p. 140); *Water Music* (p. 128)

HAYDN, Symphony No. 94 in G major (*Surprise*) (p. 265)

MONTEVERDI, *L'incoronazione di Poppea*, Act III, scene 7, Sinfonia (p. 70)

MOZART, *Le nozze di Figaro*, Overture (p. 378); Piano Concerto in G major, K. 453 (p. 309); Symphony No. 40 in G minor (p. 456)

VIVALDI, *La primavera*, from *Le quattro stagioni* (p. 98)

organ music:
   BACH, Chorale prelude, *Ein feste Burg ist unser Gott* (p. 170)

organum:
   ORGANUM, *Gaude Maria virgo* (p. 8)

ostinato: *see also* ground bass
   MONTEVERDI, *L'incoronazione di Poppea*, "Pur ti miro" (p. 71)
   PURCELL, *Dido and Aeneas*, Dido's Lament (p. 94)

overture, French:
   HANDEL, *Messiah*, Overture (p. 140)

overture from opera:
   MOZART, *Le nozze di Figaro*, Overture (p. 378)

pavane:
   SUSATO, Pavane *Mille regretz* (p. 41)

piano music:
   BEETHOVEN, Piano Sonata in C minor, Op. 13 (*Pathétique*) (p. 483)
   MOZART, Piano Sonata in A major, K. 331, III (p. 304)

polychoral music:
   GABRIELI, *O quam suavis* (p. 51)

popular tunes:
   Anonymous, *L'homme armé* tune (p. 22)
   DU FAY, *L'homme armé* Mass, Kyrie (p. 22)
   GAY, *The Beggar's Opera*, Nos. 38–40 (p. 260)

prelude:
   BACH, Prelude and Fugue in C minor (p. 199)

program music:
   VIVALDI, *La primavera*, from *Le quattro stagioni* (p. 98)

quartet, strings: *see* string quartet

recitative:
   HANDEL, *Messiah*, "There were shepherds abiding in the field" (p. 146)
   HAYDN, *Die Schöpfung*, "Und Gott sprach" (p. 287); "In vollem Glanze" (p. 288)
   MOZART, *Le nozze di Figaro*, Scene 6 (p. 378)
   PURCELL, *Dido and Aeneas*, "Thy hand, Belinda!" (p. 94)

ritornello:
   BACH, *Brandenburg Concerto* No. 2, I (p. 175)
   VIVALDI, *La primavera*, from *Le quattro stagioni* (p. 98)

rondeau:
   MACHAUT, *Puis qu'en oubli* (p. 18)

rondo:
   BEETHOVEN, Piano Sonata in C minor, Op. 13 (*Pathétique*), II (p. 490); III (p. 493); Violin Concerto in D major, Op. 61, III (p. 500)
   MOZART, *Eine kleine Nachtmusik*, II (p. 440); IV (p. 446); Piano Sonata in A major, K. 331, III (p. 304)

rounded binary form:
   MOZART, *Eine kleine Nachtmusik*, III (p. 445)

scherzo and trio:
   BEETHOVEN, Symphony No. 5 in C minor, Op. 67, III (p. 594)

serenade:
   MOZART, *Eine kleine Nachtmusik* (p. 433)

sinfonia:
   MONTEVERDI, *L'incoronazione di Poppea*, Act III, scene 7, Sinfonia (p. 70)

slow introduction: *see* introduction, slow

slow-movement sonata form:
   MOZART, *Le nozze di Figaro*, Overture (p. 378)

sonata:
   BEETHOVEN, Piano Sonata in C minor, Op. 13 (*Pathétique*) (p. 483)
   CORELLI, Trio Sonata, Op. 3, No. 2 (p. 90)
   MOZART, Piano Sonata in A major, K. 331 (p. 304)

sonata-allegro form:
BEETHOVEN, Piano Sonata in C minor, Op. 13 (*Pathétique*), I (p. 483); Symphony No. 5 in C minor, Op. 67, I (p. 524); IV (p. 594)
HAYDN, String Quartet in D minor, Op. 76, No. 2 (*Quinten*), IV (p. 278)
MOZART, *Eine kleine Nachtmusik*, I (p. 433); IV (p. 446); Symphony No. 40 in G minor, I (p. 456)
sonata da chiesa:
CORELLI, Trio Sonata, Op. 3, No. 2 (p. 90)
sonata form: *see* sonata-allegro form
sonata-rondo form: *see* rondo
string quartet:
HAYDN, String Quartet in D minor, Op. 76, No. 2 (*Quinten*) (p. 278)
MOZART, *Eine kleine Nachtmusik* (p. 433)
strophic song:
MONIOT D'ARRAS, *Ce fut en mai* (p. 14)
GAY, *The Beggar's Opera*, No. 38 (p. 260)
suite:
HANDEL, *Water Music* (p. 128)
symphony:
BEETHOVEN, Symphony No. 5 in C minor, Op. 67 (p. 524)
HAYDN, Symphony No. 94 in G major (*Surprise*) (p. 265)

MOZART, Symphony No. 40 in G minor (p. 456)
ternary form:
HANDEL, *Water Music*, Suite in D major, Allegro (p. 128); Alla hornpipe (p. 133)
MOZART, *Eine kleine Nachtmusik*, II (p. 440)
see also: da capo aria; minuet and trio; scherzo and trio
theme and variations:
BEETHOVEN, Symphony No. 5 in C minor, Op. 67, II (p. 554)
HAYDN, Symphony No. 94 in G major (*Surprise*), II (p. 265)
MOZART, Piano Concerto in G major, K. 453, III (p. 352)
see also: ground bass
three-part form: *see* ternary form
traditional music influences:
GAY, *The Beggar's Opera* (p. 260)
trio sonata:
CORELLI, Trio Sonata, Op. 3, No. 2 (p. 90)
trouvère song:
MONIOT D'ARRAS, *Ce fut en mai* (p. 14)
two-part form: *see* binary form

variations: *see* theme and variations; ground bass